PUFFIN BOOKS

Editor: Kaye Webb

PURITAN AND CAVALIER

Civil war – a nation divided against itself, with brother fighting brother. On 22 August 1642, King Charles I raised the Royal Standard at Nottingham, and the English Civil War had begun. The whole country was quickly drawn into the events that followed, and it was only six years and many bloody battles later that the Parliamentarians, under their leader Oliver Cromwell, emerged the victors. The death toll was high: 100,000 Englishmen out of a total population of 5,000,000 were killed in action in a war that most of them never wished for, but from which they could see no escape.

In this book James Barbary has written a fascinating account of the military events of the war, setting them firmly within the context of the political and religious conflicts that caused it – the long battle between King and Parliament for control of the country. He paints a vivid picture of the battles and sieges, and of the people who fought the war on both sides. *Puritan and Cavalier* is an immensely readable account of the English Civil War, and the author's tremendous grasp of detail provides an unusually exciting, graphic and personal view of one of the most formative periods of English history.

D0860636

JAMES BARBARY

Puritan
and
Cavalier

The English Civil War

PUFFIN BOOKS

Puffin Books, Penguin Books Ltd, Harmondsworth, Middlesex, England
Penguin Books, 625 Madison Avenue, New York, New York 10022, U.S.A.
Penguin Books Australia Ltd, Ringwood, Victoria, Australia
Penguin Books Canada Ltd, 2801 John Street, Markham, Ontario, Canada L3R 1B4
Penguin Books (N.Z.) Ltd, 182–190 Wairau Road, Auckland 10, New Zealand

—

First published by Victor Gollancz 1977
Published in Puffin Books 1979

—

Copyright © James Barbary, 1977
All rights reserved

—

Made and printed in Great Britain by
Hazell Watson & Viney Ltd, Aylesbury, Bucks
Set in Intertype Times Roman

Contents

England at the time of the Civil War

CHAPTER ONE

The People's Liberty

The law is the boundary, the measure, between the King's prerogative and the people's liberty, but if these bounds are removed, if the prerogative of the King overwhelm the liberty of the people, it will be turned to tyranny, if liberty undermine the prerogative, it will grow into anarchy

— JOHN PYM

A RAW, wet January afternoon in 1642. In an ancient firelit hall, under a high, beamed roof, a crowd of more than three hundred men sat uneasily along benches. Most of them were soberly dressed, and wore tall-crowned hats and plain white linen. Some were young dandies, distinctive in a glitter of braid and embroidery. But all wore sword-belts. And there they all sat, waiting on their benches in a nervous silence.

The hall was St Stephen's, Westminster, beside the River Thames, and these men were recently elected Members of Parliament, the English House of Commons. Most of the Commons were prosperous country gentlemen. Some were merchants and lawyers. And interspersed like strangers in their sombre midst were a few dozen colourful, arrogant younger men whose first loyalty in Parliament was to the Court of King Charles I and to his Queen, sparkling-eyed Henrietta Maria.

Word had come from a spy at court that this very afternoon King Charles himself was arriving at St Stephen's. He was hoping to take by surprise the five members who were the ringleaders in Parliament of opposition to his authority. King Charles was planning to charge these five men from the

Commons, and a sixth, Lord Mandeville from the House of Lords, with high treason. The penalty for treason was death.

Men sat in the House of Lords if they were bishops or if they had a hereditary peerage, but the Commons were elected. In this Parliament, most of the elected members were Puritans – sober, pious, money-making men, whose opinions both in religion and politics ran counter to the will of the King.

John Pym, a square, well-fed man of fifty-eight, with a confident smile and a little chin beard, was their leader, and all eyes were on him. Pym was a man of cold nerve and clear vision – a consummate political organizer. He had been a boy in Devon when memories of how the Elizabethan sea-dogs had singed King Philip's beard and raided the Spanish Main were still vividly alive. To John Pym, Parliament represented the best side of England, and Roman Catholics, in the King's court and in Ireland, were still the national enemy.

In the election that had brought this Puritan majority triumphantly to Parliament, John Pym had organized his followers with the smiling and energetic competence of an Elizabethan sea captain. He had ridden on horseback the length and breadth of England, praying with the religious Puritans, arguing politics with the discontented ones, and at need bribing voters with huge feasts or beef and beer.

And now King Charles, after managing to govern England for eleven years (1629–40) without a Parliament, would be faced this afternoon in the great hall of St Stephen's – where laws were made and taxes decided – with an array of his determined enemies.

The King's palace of Whitehall was only a few hundred yards away from Parliament. King Charles came through the door of his palace and stepped into the royal coach. Around him rode a brave cavalry escort of several hundred guards and gentlemen pensioners, brisk young sprigs of noble family, extravagant in their dress and laughing and confident in their demeanour.

The King was forty-two years old. His features were obstinately set, and he was dressed with rich sobriety. Today he had almost changed his mind at the last moment about the wisdom of arresting the Five Members – changing his mind was a besetting fault with King Charles – but the high-spirited Queen had taunted him to his face. Pym was Henrietta Maria's enemy, and she wanted to see his head cut off.

As King Charles got down from his coach and strode into firelit St Stephen's, the gay gentlemen of his armed escort pushed the door of the great hall wide open and crowded the doorway threateningly. Some cocked their pistols and pretended to take aim at members they particularly disliked. But the five members of the Commons they hated the most had gone.

John Pym, leader of the five, was the brains of the opposition. Another of them was John Hampden, a rich Buckinghamshire landowner, who had already run the risk of prison rather than pay a royal tax called Ship Money, which he judged to be illegal. Another was a wealthy Puritan called Denzil Holles. Arthur Haselrig, the fourth, had angered King Charles by proposing that officers in the army and navy should be appointed, not by the King, but by Parliament. The fifth was William Strode, son of a West Country clothier, who after defying the King in an earlier Parliament had been sent to prison for eleven grim years.

The Five Members had lingered in their places until the King's horsemen came clattering into Palace Yard. Then, putting on cloaks against the cold, they had hastened with Lord Mandeville to the Water Gate, where a boat was moored, with oarsmen ready to take them downriver to a secret refuge in the City.

At the last moment, the others had been obliged to take William Strode by the arms and drag him away to the Water Gate by force. Eleven years in prison had made him angry, he now wanted to stand there and brave King Charles face to face. But that was not what John Pym had in mind. His scheme was to show up the King publicly, and in the most striking way, as a monarch with no respect for law and order. Highly strung, dignified, and cold in manner, Charles began to stalk across the floor of the House towards the Speaker's chair. Watched by all eyes the King paused to take off his hat. At this royal courtesy, all the members present rose to their feet and did the same, standing there bareheaded.

Solemnly, and one by one, King Charles asked for the Five Members accused of high treason.

'Is Mr Pym here?'

Silence.

'Is Mr Hampden here?'

Silence.

'Is Mr Holles here?'

Silence to each name in turn.

Turning to face the Speaker, the King then asked him directly to say if the Five Members were present. Speaker Lenthall, bookish, a lawyer by profession and notoriously prone to take bribes, fell timidly to his knees, but managed at this great moment to find the right words for his refusal to answer.

'May it please Your Majesty, I have neither eyes to see nor tongue to speak in this place, but as this House is pleased to direct me, whose servant I am.'

' 'Tis no matter,' said King Charles, his slightly stammering voice, high-pitched and impatient, holding a trace of a Scottish accent. 'I think my eyes are as good as another's.' His gaze moved along the rows of men. A few there he could recognize as his friends. Most of those dark-clad, middle-aged men were his implacable enemies, though all stood there respectfully bareheaded before him. With a kind of forlorn anger, the King at last said loudly, 'All my birds are flown.'

King Charles had hoped, this afternoon, to silence opposition in Parliament by one quick and terrifying act, but force had failed him. In the eyes of an influential part of England – the God-fearing, Bible-reading, busily prosperous part, the men whom their opponents had nicknamed Puritans – the King had put himself hopelessly in the wrong.

England, like most other countries in Europe, had been ruled by a king since time immemorial. For many Englishmen their first loyalty, come what may, was to the King. But those Englishmen who had voted the Puritan majority into this Parliament were turning against the King's arbitrary rule.

They wanted Parliament to exercise the supreme authority in the realm, and they hoped that because of their votes and their influence they would have a share in this authority. The conflict over who should govern England, and in what way, was now so sharp it could probably be resolved only by force of arms. England that cold afternoon was but one step away from civil war.

In 1642, only one fifth of the peers who sat by hereditary right in the House of Lords and helped to make the laws had ever served in a war. They were no longer an ancient and warlike feudal aristocracy. In fact, nearly two-thirds of the families had not borne their titles for longer than thirty years. Some of them were aristocrats of a new breed, courtiers who not long since had bought their rank with money. Between 1603 and 1625, when his son Charles came to the throne and stopped the malpractice, King James I had amassed no less than £620,000 by selling titles of honour to rich men for hard cash.

King Charles, too, was always short of money. Even in

times of peace, the King's income was scarcely enough to meet the expenses of his government. Other kings in Europe could enforce their authority by a standing army, but an army is costly, and Charles never had the money to pay more than a handful of soldiers. England had the lowest taxes in Europe, and they could not be increased without the consent of a Parliament.

Being short of money, King Charles was driven to rewarding his courtiers as best he could. Often he gave them commercial privileges. Lord Goring, for example, was allowed to take a percentage from sugar imports and butter exports. Endymion Porter, who bought pictures for the royal art-collection, had been repaid by King Charles with a monopoly of white writing paper.

So any thrifty and hard-working person in London who sweetened his pudding with sugar, or spread his bread with butter, or even wrote a letter, made his small contribution to the income of some extravagant courtier. Clever politicians like John Pym had been teaching the people of London to resent bitterly this kind of simple but unpleasant fact.

Charles had never wanted to be King. The Crown had come his way unexpectedly when his elder brother Henry died. But King Charles, though sometimes pushed to extremes by the courtiers who were his advisers, was a deeply conscientious man, who believed that he should rule as the father of his people, and that this right had been granted him by God. Parliament might begrudge him money to pay an army and to use force, but he hoped to rule in men's hearts.

King Charles had tried, by fits and starts, to watch out for the interests of his poorer and unluckier subjects. This, too, had separated him from the Puritans, who despised the poor and thought poverty a mark of God's disfavour. Charles had encouraged his bishops and judges to enforce laws that would keep the wages of poor weavers from being cut to starvation level when times were hard. He tried to stop go-ahead landowners from enclosing common lands and village fields, because when fields were enclosed the poor cottagers lost their livelihood and had to beg for their bread on the highway. Many enterprising Puritans who paid low wages or were not above filching common lands loved King Charles and his bishops the less for this interference. And though to celebrate a Roman Catholic mass in England was then a serious crime, Charles, at the urging of his Catholic Queen, Henrietta Maria, had begun to allow his many Roman Catholic subjects to worship in the way they chose. The Puritans particularly hated him for that.

'People are governed,' King Charles once said, 'more by the pulpit than the sword, in times of peace.' He knew that the Church of England, the only church allowed in his realm by law, would always speak out for the King. In those days, every Englishman was legally obliged to attend service in his parish church on Sundays. The bishops censored the press, so church was where most people got their news and formed their opinions. In those days controlling the church was as important to the government – and to the opposition – as ownership of newspapers or television would be now.

The Puritan majority in Parliament had begun to hope that a Presbyterian system of church government would destroy the King's influence over the church and place it directly under their own control. Disagreements over religion were deep in England and went back a hundred years, to the time when Henry VIII, having refused obedience to the Pope, began to share out the lands of the Roman Catholic Church in England amongst his supporters.

When King Henry's daughter Mary I, nicknamed Bloody Mary, came to the throne with a Spanish prince for a husband and tried to restore the authority of the Roman Catholic

Church, men who had come into possession of church lands feared for their estates. But in those years many ordinary people also became anti-Catholic, especially in London, where they had seen Protestants who refused to give up their faith being burned at the stake at Smithfield.

Hundreds of Protestant gentlemen and clergy went abroad in Bloody Mary's time to save their lives. Many of these exiles sought refuge in Geneva, a Protestant city-state governed according to the ideas of John Calvin.

These English exiles liked what they saw in Geneva. Neither King nor Pope had any say in the running of John Calvin's church. In every parish, the more substantial men were the church elders, and they shared authority with the minister. The city magistrate was there to punish those who were irreligious. The system was so well-organized that no disbeliever dared raise his head.

When Mary died in 1558, her sister Elizabeth gained the throne, and English Protestants could breathe freely once more. Some of the Calvinist exiles crowding back home rose into prominence as the new Queen's advisers. Calvin's strict system of church government – Presbyterianism – was already being adopted in the sister kingdom of Scotland. The Queen's Calvinist advisers wanted to see England follow Scotland's example.

But Elizabeth was too wise a Queen for that. She well knew that most of her subjects kept a lingering belief in the sacraments of the Old Religion and preferred an easy-going life both on weekdays and Sundays.

So Elizabeth organized the Church of England on Episcopalian lines, controlling it through her own bishops, who had political authority because of their seats in the House of Lords. She wanted to make the Church of England so comprehensive that no zealous minority would be able to impose its particular will. She hoped to see almost any believing

Englishman, from an old-fashioned Catholic to a strict Calvinist – not to mention all the many good people in between these two extremes – attend Sunday service cheerfully in his own parish church without too much of a wrench.

After Queen Elizabeth's death in 1603, the Scottish King, James, inherited her throne. He was less skilful at keeping the English united and satisfied. King James bore down hard on the Puritans, and offended Parliament. He raised a resentment against arbitrary actions by the Crown that his son Charles, who followed his father's ways, was less and less able to control.

Charles inherited the throne in 1625. He was a religious man and identified himself fervently with the Church of England. During the eleven years when he reigned without calling a Parliament, his Archbishop, William Laud, began to persecute Puritan dissenters, and to use the church deliberately as a moral reinforcement of the King's authority.

In the City of London, as in many of the country towns now busy with the cloth trade, the Presbyterians, as those wanting John Calvin's system of church organization were now generally called, often had a substantial following. But in most of the English countryside, they were held in contempt.

At the time when the Five Members fled to the City of London for refuge, one man in three there was still a Royalist, even though the City was considered a Puritan stronghold. In the suburbs of London, where the poorer people lived, four men in five were thought to favour the King. Pym had managed the election to Parliament of a Puritan majority, but even where he had gained the most votes, his convinced supporters, though often wealthy, intelligent, and well organized, could find themselves outnumbered by those who for one reason or another were content to let the King go on ruling.

Nor was everyone nicknamed 'Puritan' a Presbyterian.

Certain Puritans, from the great poet and scholar John Milton to humble shopkeepers and craftsmen and small farmers, wanted to worship in a church free from all control by bishop or magistrate. They were called Independents. Because churches of the kind they favoured had already been founded by like-minded Puritans across the Atlantic, the Independent system of church government was often known as the New England Way.

By the time King Charles stalked into Parliament to arrest John Pym and his friends and send them to the scaffold, the differences between Parliament and King had become irreconcilable. The King would not give up the essentials of his sovereignty, yet on its own account Parliament obstinately demanded a full share of real power. The most serious of the differences bringing King and Parliament into violent collision was over which of them should control England's army, and therefore the ultimate source of authority in the realm, the actual brute force.

But those who sought power in the state wanted also to

English Pike Exercise 1: Advance your pike – the pikeman holds the butt in his right hand (National Army Museum)

manipulate the invisible but potent influence over men's minds that organized religion would give them. They fought to determine how the church in England should be organized and controlled. So when men took sides in the civil war, their loyalty usually reflected their religious belief. Anglicans of the King's party were ready to tolerate Roman Catholics, yet were violently opposed to those who wanted a Presbyterian system of church government. The Presbyterians themselves were deeply mistrusted by those extreme Puritans called Independents.

Religious groupings soon began to act like political parties, especially on the Parliamentary side. Men who cared little for religion might for political reasons call themselves, say, 'Presbyterian', yet act in ways that any sincere church-going Presbyterian then or since would find repulsive.

The threatening civil war would also turn out in the end to have been fought for land.

Not all the land belonging of old to the church had yet been shared out. The Puritans in Parliament found themselves sorely tempted by cathedral and Crown estates, as well as by

English Pike Exercise 2: Shoulder your pike, first motion – the pikeman lowers the butt, grasps the pike high up with his left hand (National Army Museum)

common fields and royal forests. Some of the King's opponents wanted trade freed from court interference. But above all, their hope of buying up more land if they won, and their fear of losing their estates as rebels if they lost, spurred to extremes not a few of the Puritan gentlemen who sat in John Pym's Parliament.

That cold January night in 1642, the Five Members hid in Coleman Street, where every house was Puritan. The City was wild with excitement at the dramatic escape of the Five Members. Ministers preached long sermons from fiery biblical texts, justifying resistance to King Charles, and even hinting at civil war. 'To your tents, O Israel!' they exclaimed that Sunday from the pulpit. All London sensed that a critical moment had come.

The tradesmen and craftsmen who worked in their little shops in the alleys off Coleman Street – and particularly their young apprentices – were all ready to fight for their beliefs, and had been busy learning how.

For lack of a standing army, England was defended in those days by a volunteer militia. In counties a long way from

English Pike Exercise 3: Shoulder your pike, second motion – the pikeman moves his right hand from the butt to as far up as he can reach (National Army Museum)

London, militiamen were usually loyal to the King. But these county volunteers were half-hearted soldiers. They trained once a month, in summer, and after shooting off a couple of musket shots at a target, they would troop away to the nearest tavern. But in London, the fifteen thousand volunteers of the City's trained bands took their amateur soldiering in earnest.

They had not long since been put under the command of a trusty professional officer, Philip Skippon, a good-hearted veteran and convinced Presbyterian, who had risen on merit in the Dutch service from private soldier to general. When the crisis came, Skippon and his men could be relied upon to fight for Parliament. And except for the King's personal body-guard and the seamen of the Royal Navy, the trained bands of the City were the only efficient fighting men now in England.

Philip Skippon would unquestionably bring over the trained bands to fight for Parliament, and another close friend of John Pym's, Robert Rich, the Earl of Warwick, could be relied on to make sure of the navy.

Though the Earl of Warwick was numbered politically among the Puritans, there was nothing very pure about him.

English Pike Exercise 4: Shoulder your pike, third motion – the long and heavy pike rests at last on the pikeman's shoulder (National Army Museum)

He was a foul-mouthed reckless man, with a full beard and the manners of an old sea-dog. 'Foremost in fight, capable of climbing mast and yard,' he had made money by organizing piracy off the Spanish Main. In 1618, his father had bought the title to the ancient earldom of Warwick for £10,000, cash down.

Besides piracy, the Earl's other great interest was helping Puritans emigrate to America. In recent years, twenty thousand Englishmen had gone to make a better life for themselves across the Atlantic in the New World. Warwick had done much to organize this vast emigration. He had aided the Pilgrim Fathers who sailed in the *Mayflower*, and with his friend Pym, he sponsored emigration to Connecticut and Rhode Island. But Warwick also showed the other, more piratical, side of his character when he became the first Englishman to ship black slaves to Virginia. The sea-dog Earl of Warwick was very popular with sailors in the port of London, so the navy would follow his lead. Once he heard that the Five Members had safely escaped he collected two thousand seamen from Ratcliffe and Wapping in the port of London, and marched them in procession through the streets of the City to offer their services in the Parliamentary cause. The trained bands came out in their thousands. The Five Members were rowed back triumphantly up the Thames to Westminster, and along each bank, as escort, marched Philip Skippon's men, with banners flying and trumpets resounding.

The King was being publicly reminded who it was that controlled the armed power in his own capital. If he went on throwing down a challenge to Parliament, King Charles would have to create a navy and an army of his own, beginning from scratch. 'How is it I have lost the hearts of these water rats?' King Charles exclaimed when he heard that the men of the Royal Navy had pledged to fight for Parliament. One simple answer sufficed. Money from the royal treasury, better spent on buying the navy's loyalty, had been frittered away in extravagant pensions to court favourites. In the King's ships, there were seamen who had not touched a penny of their pay for seven years.

In his heart King Charles sensed that he had lost London to his enemies. The royal family no longer felt safe there. Their eldest daughter, Mary, was engaged to marry the Prince of Orange, and Charles and James were boys. Therefore, on the night of 10 January 1642, the King impulsively fled from Whitehall Palace with Queen Henrietta Maria and these three older children. The two youngest royal children, Henry and Elizabeth, fell into the hands of Parliament, and were kept as hostages.

King Charles and his family reached Hampton late that night. Hampton Court Palace, about twelve miles south-west of London, was the first stage of the King's journey. They all undressed in the dark and slept together in the same bed.

The year 1642 was to become a period of decision, with everyone in England sensing a need to take sides. Yet all but a few fanatics would have been content with a decorative and obliging King who made things easier for everyone by handing over his more important powers to Parliament.

Charles, however, had been taught as a boy that his powers and duties had been entrusted to him by God. Sometimes, when hard pressed, he would go through the motions of bargaining, but he would never let go the essence of his authority. He was King of all his people, including the Roman Catholics and the poor. He ruled his kingdom in accordance with God's will, and on these essentials, nothing could make him change or yield.

In early February, King Charles took his Queen and their eldest daughter, Mary, down to Dover. Queen Henrietta

Maria was a high-spirited Frenchwoman with black eyes, dark ringlets, and a flashing smile. She had inherited the imperious will and cheerful courage of her royal father, Henry IV of France and Navarre. And she was displaying courage now. Hidden away in the Queen's baggage were the Crown Jewels of England.

Henrietta Maria's plan was to take the jewels to Holland and pawn them there to raise money and buy arms for the King. On the day she finally parted with them, she wrote to him, 'They looked so handsome, I assure you I gave them up with no small regret.'

Waiting for the King and Queen at Dover was a huge, broad-shouldered, swarthy young nephew of the King, called Rupert, the younger son of Charles's sister Elizabeth, the exiled Queen of Bohemia. He had crossed the Channel to serve King Charles as a soldier.

Prince Rupert had gone off to the wars when he was only thirteen. At nineteen, when serving as a colonel in Germany, the young prince had been captured at the battle of Vlotho. For the next three years he was locked up in an imperial fortress, with a large white poodle called Boy as his friend and companion.

Prince Rupert spent those years of imprisonment in a zealous study of the art of war. He had been let out of the fortress only two months before, and now was ready to go to war again, this time in the service of his uncle, King Charles.

At the King's suggestion, Rupert turned back at Dover to escort the Queen and Princess Mary – and the Crown Jewels – safely to Holland. The young Prince was next seen later that year off the English coast as he stood on the deck of a hired Dutch merchantman off Flamborough Head, his long black ringlets hidden from sight under a seaman's cap. Crammed under the ship's hatches were muskets and powder for the King.

Prince Rupert dodged three Parliamentary men-of-war and managed to run his cargo of arms ashore into the little port of Tynemouth. He then rode off on his charger, with his white poodle Boy at his heels, to join his uncle and lead the royal cavalry in battle.

London then had 400,000 inhabitants and was by far the biggest, richest, and most important city in England. The second largest city in the kingdom, Bristol, numbered only 25,000.

Royalists living in counties near London – in Kent, Essex, and Sussex – did not stand much chance when the King fled his capital, because their county militia declared for Parliament, and their stores of arms were seized. But on the fringes of the kingdom, where life was poor, harsh, and traditional, in Cornwall, Wales, and Northumberland, far from commercial London, the counties declared for the King.

Soon a line could be drawn across the map of England. Parliament's heartland was in the south and east, spreading outwards from London and East Anglia. The King's friends had established their authority across the countryside in the north and west.

But even in these Royalist counties, the small towns were often Puritan. Soon they were besieged, and the civil war in these areas became a war between town and country. The Puritan port-towns held out best, because the Earl of Warwick's ships could supply them. The Yorkshire port of Hull, though long-besieged, was a stronghold for Parliament, and so was Plymouth in the west. A gallant young Presbyterian soldier called Edward Massey fortified Gloucester, at the crossing over the River Severn, and managed to hold it, even though Gloucester could not be supplied by sea.

In the heart of Parliamentary territory, a handful of people living in private castles and fortified mansion houses stood foursquare for the King. Newark Castle and Basing House, for instance, were able to threaten the main roads north and west from London.

And so Parliament's conflict with the King soon drifted into a civil war with no fixed front, where neighbour was often at war with neighbour, and sometimes brother fought brother – a. war that most Englishmen certainly never wished for, but from which they could see no way to escape.

Up in Lancashire, five thousand people then lived in a small town called Manchester, where weavers from the villages around brought their cloth to market. Most men in the cloth trade were Puritan, though the Lancashire countryside was overwhelmingly Royalist, and often Roman Catholic.

James Stanley, Lord Strange, soon to be the seventh Earl of Derby, was the richest of the Lancashire landowners. His lordship was arrogant, cruel, and cowardly, and he was important only because he was a man of great possessions. For those he considered his enemies – the Puritan weavers, busy in the little towns – he had a bitter contempt.

In September 1642, his lordship mustered at Warrington over two thousand men loyal to the King. The Manchester clothiers meanwhile, well aware they were threatened, had offered £60 a year to a German soldier called Johann Rosworm to put their little township in a state of defence.

Rosworm soon got the citizens building mud walls at the street ends, and he hung chains from house to house to impede cavalry charges. Men who had spent all their lives working indoors at the loom eagerly began to learn the use of pike and musket.

Lord Derby and his horsemen showed up outside Manchester on a wet Sunday. The bells in the parish church rang a warning. The citizens tumbled out of church and ran eagerly for their weapons, though outnumbered three to one. The best marksmen were placed up in the church tower as sharp-shooters.

The charging Royalists, as they galloped headlong at the mud barricades, were held there and driven back by weavers thrusting home-made pikes. In the midst of battle, the Manchester men sang psalms, and as they stood in the drizzle at the blocked street-ends waiting for the next attack, they prayed aloud to keep their spirits up.

After six days of desperate warfare, in endless pouring rain, Lord Derby decamped, leaving two hundred dead behind him. The Manchester men were down to their last six pounds of gunpowder – but they had won.

There were similar little Puritan clothing towns across the Pennines, in Yorkshire. At first the gentry of Yorkshire, both Puritan and Royalist, tried to reach a neighbourly agreement to keep their county neutral in the threatening war. But from further north, a Royalist army under William Cavendish, Lord Newcastle, began to move down upon them.

The Yorkshire weavers had a champion of their own in young Sir Thomas Fairfax of Nunappleton House. Tom Fairfax's grandfather had been a famous general in Elizabethan times. Fairfax himself, like many other young men of his day, had gone off to gain experience and have adventures in a brief campaign on the Protestant side in the Dutch Wars.

He had married a soldier's daughter – plain, forthright, a fervent Presbyterian. For his service in the brief and badly handled war against the Scots, when King Charles was defeated in his intention of imposing the Anglican form of prayer on the Scots by force, Tom Fairfax had been knighted.

But Fairfax's military experience so far did not amount to much, and he entered the Civil War as an amateur soldier. He was simply the young man whom his neighbours among the Puritan gentry of Yorkshire were glad to follow on horse-back – the sweet-natured, unselfish, sublimely courageous leader of irregular cavalry to whom the poor weavers of Yorkshire turned when their way of life was threatened by Royalist forays. The admiring Yorkshiremen nicknamed him Black Tom, and eventually Black Tom Fairfax became Parliament's most famous and effective soldier.

CHAPTER TWO

For King or for the Commonweal

For King or for the Commonweal –
No matter which they say,
The first dry rattle of new-drawn steel
Changes the world today!
— RUDYARD KIPLING, *Edgehill Fight*

AT Nottingham, King Charles raised the Royal Standard, the traditional feudal sign that a King of England was calling up his loyal retainers.

Though the King had no regular army, many of the country gentlemen who rallied with such high hearts to his banner had already gained some experience in waging war on the continent of Europe. In the Low Countries there had been a long-drawn-out war between the Protestant Dutch and Catholic Spain, which had lasted on and off for a man's lifetime. Many Protestant Englishmen had taken a hand for the Dutch, and some of the King's Roman Catholic subjects had fought on the side of Spain.

There had been English volunteers too in Germany, during the Thirty Years' War, the best of them fighting in the romantic but helpless cause of Prince Rupert's mother, the exiled Queen of Bohemia. To see a little of a continental war was at that time thought to be a proper thing for an English gentleman to do.

Rupert, young though he was, had fought in both the Dutch and German wars, so that when, as his uncle's General of Horse, he was given the job of making an efficient cavalry out of a mixed crowd of gay courtiers, fox-hunting country gentlemen, and their loyal tenantry, he soon found himself amid a troop of friends. Most of them knew how to ride a horse full tilt at a hedge and could fire off a pistol, but from the first, the royal cavalry was inclined to be resentful about being given strict orders. In the King's army there were already too many officers, and not enough men in the ranks.

Sixty or so men under a captain formed a troop of cavalry in those days, with six or more troops making up a regiment, under a colonel. When they went into action, cavalrymen wore helmets, but at other times they wore broad-brimmed felt hats that kept off the rain. Some had breast plates, but their chief protection in battle was a thick buffcoat of dressed bullhide, capable of turning a sword-thrust.

Cavalrymen rather looked down their noses at dragoons, who were a kind of infantry on horseback. In battle, the dragoons fought dismounted and protected the army's flanks or harried a cavalry charge by firing off their carbines from behind a hedge.

The 'poor foot' – pikemen and musketeers – marched under a weight of eighty pounds or more. When they were lucky, they got rations at the rate of half a pound of cheese and a pound of bread per day. Ten miles along muddy English lanes was an average day's march for these heavily burdened infantrymen. The guns made the going even slower. In fact, except for knocking down walls in sieges, the clumsy and inaccurate cannon of those days were almost more nuisance than they were worth.

The King offered footsoldiers the same money as field labourers – eightpence to tenpence a day – but he was often not able to pay them. Welshmen, however, flocked in to serve. They were passionately Royalist, but also so poor that even the offchance of getting eightpence a day was worth taking.

Because the King's army was irregularly paid, a new word had recently entered the English language: *plunder*. What the

A musketeer charges his musket barrel from his powder flask before ramming down the ball (John Freeman)

King's troops lacked they took by force, and the joke began to spread among the Royalists that 'every rich man we pass is a Roundhead.'

The strongest footsoldiers were given pikes. These were immensely long spears, with an ash stave three times the height of a man, which were lowered in ranks to present a forest of blades to the enemy. The musketeers usually fought in files six deep, in gaps between the solid blocks of pikemen, or else they were sent out in front, as sharp-shooters, to take the brunt of the enemy's first charge.

Musketeers were armed with a firelock with a four-foot barrel that was so heavy that at close quarters it made a good club. The firelock could send a lead ball weighing one ounce a distance of four hundred yards, but any musketeer who could hit his man at sixty yards was reckoned a crack shot. Loading took so long that a musketeer had to be well trained to get off three shots in a minute.

In King Charles's makeshift army, now marching from Shrewsbury towards London, muskets had been so hard to come by that several hundred of the newly enlisted foot soldiers were armed with cudgels. Only horsemen in the front rank wore breast plates, and only a lucky few had pistols, carbines, or sporting guns.

Young Prince Rupert led the royal cavalry, already nicknamed Cavaliers because of their resemblance to the pillaging Spanish *caballeros* who had fought and plundered in the Low Countries. Sir Jacob Astley, a quiet little old Roman Catholic gentleman of great experience, commanded the royal foot.

And what was to stop the King's men from marching now on London and restoring Charles to his throne? Only a hastily-organized Parliamentary army, under the Earl of Essex.

Robert Devereux, third Earl of Essex, a big, slow-moving man of fifty-one, was another Puritan peer. He was fond of smoking a long clay pipe, was brave, trustworthy, and liked by his men, but was not a rapid thinker, and his dispatches, written in big, clumsy letters and badly spelled, show that he was not quick with a pen, either. As a young man, Essex had

A musketeer thrusts ball and powder home with his ramrod (John Freeman)

led a troop of cavalry in the continental wars, but he had never commanded a regiment there, much less fought a battle.

Some of his regimental officers had even less experience. They were middle-aged Puritan members of Parliament, who were learning the art of war from scratch. John Hampden, one of the Five Members, had raised a regiment of volunteer infantry from his Buckinghamshire estates and put them into green uniforms. Another of the Five, Denzil Holles, had raised his own regiment too, but dressed his men bravely in red. Otherwise, in both armies, most soldiers wore what they chose.

A heavy-bodied, brooding-eyed man of forty-three, who had been Member of Parliament for Cambridge, was serving in the Puritan army as captain of cavalry. He was John Hampden's little-known country cousin, Oliver Cromwell, a man who lived by the Bible and spent much time in prayer, a cattle-farmer from the Fens.

To the first pitched battle of the Civil War Oliver Cromwell led a mounted troop of his Puritan neighbours from East Anglia, and though he was a middle-aged politician, learning the art of war as he went along, Cromwell, like Black Tom Fairfax, was soon to rise to greatness as a soldier.

The Parliamentary foot soldiers were good and bad, mixed together. The best among them were London apprentices from the trained bands who had volunteered to follow Essex. Their cropped hair, at a time when most men wore their hair long, had already given the Parliamentarians the nickname of Roundheads. But far too many of Lord Essex's foot-soldiers were the London unemployed, for whom any service was better than the life of poverty they had left behind. They were men who had little heart for the fight, but they had not been slow to learn the significance of that useful new word: *plunder.*

*

As King Charles's army, that bright but cold October of 1642, moved deliberately through the autumnal landscape from Shropshire towards London, the Earl of Essex and his men were also on the march, feeling their way across country, trying to block the King's route.

Officers in the Parliamentary army were getting ready for morning service in the parish church of Kineton, a village in Warwickshire, when word came that King Charles and his men were only a couple of miles off. The royal army could be seen on the skyline, deployed along Edgehill, a three-mile ridge of high ground to the south-east, across the road to London. Instead of Lord Essex blocking the King's way to London, King Charles was obstructing Essex. To get home to their base, the Parliamentary army would have to fight for it.

The Earl of Essex at this moment had no wish to give battle. His guns were stuck in the mud, somewhere to the rear, and a whole brigade of horse and foot, including Hampden's greencoats and Cromwell's Fenmen, had not yet come up to join him. But this challenging royal manoeuvre – sitting up there on Edgehill and blocking his road home – gave Lord Essex little choice except to fight.

At this early stage in the war, most men believed that after one big battle between the King and his enemies, all would be decided.

The two most heart-whole and excited Royalists that day were Charles, Prince of Wales, aged twelve, and his younger brother James, Duke of York, who was only nine – both of them, later, to become Kings of England. From the top of Edgehill, they could see Essex and his Roundhead army moving towards them from Kineton. Then, on a broad plain below Edgehill, and about a mile and a half off, the enemy soldiers turned from their column of march and slowly formed into a battle line. The centre of the Parliamentary army consisted of footsoldiers, drawn up in three brigades. Each brigade was made up of solid blocks of pikemen, with musketeers standing in the gaps between them and spread out in front as skirmishers. To the left and right, on each flank, were the Parliamentary cavalry.

The young princes were taken to the King's tent, where their father, dressed in a black cloak lined with ermine, was speaking his mind to royal officers who had crowded in to hear him. There had been a prudent attempt to keep King Charles well away from the danger of battle, but he would have none of it. 'Your King is both your cause, your quarrel and your captain,' he told the crowd of officers. 'Come life or death, your King will bear you company.' Watched by his sons, Charles then put on helmet and armour and went down the hill to his place at the head of his guardsmen in the cavalry reserve.

The entire royal army was scrambling pell mell down the steep descent of Edgehill towards the broad field where Essex and his men had offered battle. Young Charles and his brother James managed to slip away and join them.

They watched the royal artillerymen move the two heaviest guns downhill – a risky business. These were demi-cannon, each weighing 4,000 pounds, and able to throw a 27-pound ball. They were lowered down the perilous slope by rope traces fastened to the harness of eight huge cart-horses, hauling against the deadweight in tandem. The big horses stood lurching and scuffling, leaning the strength of their bodies breathlessly against the weight of iron.

And so they went all the way downhill to where the royal army was forming up in a battle line, with the footsoldiers, under Sir Jacob Astley, a solid block in the centre, and Prince Rupert's horsemen to left and right on the wings.

Young Charles got hold of an unloaded pistol, and was caught out in front of the royal line, snapping the trigger at

the Roundheads and shouting 'I fear them not!' He and
James were then hustled up Edgehill to safety, but from the
crest of the hill they could still see all that was going on.

Six long hours were spent forming up the royal army on the
plain under Edgehill – drummer boys beating commands,
colours flapping in the chill breeze, sergeants shouting
hoarsely and pushing the inexperienced royal soldiers into
line with well-judged shoves of their halberds.

At last the soldiers on both sides were brought close enough
to see the faces of the foe. On the right wing Prince Rupert,
a giant on horseback, headed a double line of impatient royal
cavalry. Rupert's second line was formed by Sir John Byron's
regiment, equipped for the King at a cost of £5,000 by Lord
Worcester, a rich Roman Catholic peer. Byron's regiment
included in its ranks three hundred hot-headed students from
Oxford, who had left their quiet libraries only a few weeks
before and now were eager for the fray.

By one o'clock in the afternoon, the two armies were only
two hundred yards apart, and they looked remarkably alike,
except that as a field sign all the Parliament men wore orange
scarves. As the guns on both sides opened fire, the two young
princes, from their vantage point on Edgehill, could see
enemy cannonballs thud and ricochet into the hillside beneath
them, so that the ground trembled under their feet.

The King's two huge demi-cannon, tilted on gun-carriages
behind the royal line, began lobbing 27-pound shot right over
the heads of Sir Jacob Astley's infantry, higher than their tall
pikestaves, so that they dropped amid the facing ranks of
enemy foot. Roundhead musketeers were moving out towards
the royal lines. The battle had begun.

Against those musketeers, Prince Rupert sent out dragoons,
commanded by a bold and trustworthy officer, Lieutenant-
Colonel Henry Washington (a collateral ancestor of George

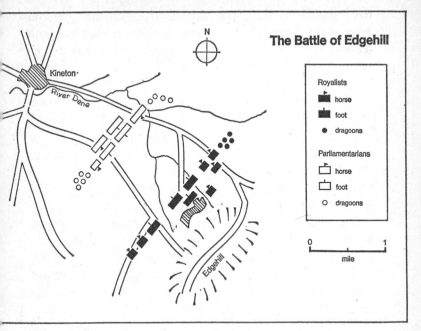

The battlefield at Edgehill, 23 October 1642

Washington). Once the Roundhead skirmishers had been pushed aside, Rupert rose, gigantic in his stirrups, and, raising his arm, gave the signal for the Cavaliers on the right flank to charge.

The young princes saw their adored cousin Rupert gallop diagonally across the battlefield at the head of his men, black ringlets and red cloak streaming, his poodle Boy running like an uncanny white spirit at his charger's heels. Waving swords and brandishing pistols, the front-line cavalry on the royal right flank followed Rupert closely, increasing their pace from a fast trot to a full gallop.

The second line, including those madcap Oxford students, had no business whatever joining in this charge. They should have waited for the word of command. But there was no holding them back. Every single Cavalier on the right flank thundered away after Rupert, leaving Sir Jacob Astley's infantry stripped on that side of cavalry cover, and naked to attack.

At the first impact out there on the plain, swords flashed, pistols cracked, smoke drifted like haze across the autumn field. From up on the hill, the excited young princes saw four entire regiments of Parliamentary foot break at the crash of Rupert's charge, and run without firing a shot – gentlemen on horseback scattering like snipe a mob of unemployed Londoners who scarcely knew how to load a musket.

On the flank against which Rupert struck, the Parliamentary horsemen were also badly shaken, but as much by an act of treachery in their own ranks as by the onset of the charging Cavaliers. One troop of horsemen in the Parliamentary ranks, recently brought over from Ireland from the army fighting the Catholic Irish rebels, was commanded by Sir Faithful Fortescue. He had secretly pledged that in the moment of battle he would bring his men over to the King's side. As Rupert's cavalry came up at the gallop, the men of Fortescue's troop fired their pistols into the ground, tore off their orange scarves, and wheeled to join the Cavaliers.

This act of desertion, followed by the terrifying impact of Rupert's charge, swept away in confusion the Parliamentary cavalry on that side of the field.

The Cavaliers on the left of the royal line had by now also charged en masse, throwing the Parliamentary horse there into much the same confusion, but they had left old Sir Jacob Astley with not a single horseman to cover either of his flanks from attack.

There was no stopping the royal cavalry once it got going. From Edgehill the two young princes could see the entire force of Cavaliers from both wings of the royal battle-line sweep onwards past the ranks of the foe, until they were mere specks in the distance.

Some reached Kineton village and were beginning to plunder the cottages, when John Hampden's greencoats came up the road and drove them back.

The first blows in the battle of Edgehill had clearly gone to the King.

Now that he had no horsemen whatever to cover his flanks, old Sir Jacob Astley knew that his best chance lay in attack. Giving his men the order to lower pikes, he knelt in front of them in prayer and said aloud 'O Lord, Thou knowest how busy I must be this day. If I forget Thee, do not Thou forget me.' Then he rose to his feet, a little white-haired man of sixty-three, waved his arm, and shouted cheerfully 'March on, boys!'

The sight of these Royalist pikemen, their weapons lowered and coming towards them at the charge, was too much for the centre brigade of Parliamentary foot. Without waiting for the push of the pikes, they broke in panic. At this desperate moment in the battle, the Puritan Earl of Essex is said to have snatched up a pike himself, and fought shoulder to shoulder with the loyal handful who stood their ground.

There were steady Parliamentary infantry still on the field – the regiments from Essex and London, with unshakeable Puritans and crop-headed, high-spirited apprentice lads in their ranks. And unlike the Cavaliers, Lord Essex had not thrown away his entire force of cavalry in wild, undisciplined charges. This restraint served him well.

To plug the hole in his centre, Essex brought up two small regiments of cavalry from the reserve. Of the forty-two troops of Parliamentary horse that had begun the battle, only fifteen were still on the field, but their readiness to fight turned the tide.

*

One of the many common folk seeing war that day for the first time in his life was a Londoner called John Okey, thirty-six years old, who was serving as quartermaster to a troop of horse commanded by another Puritan peer, Lord Brooke. John Okey was more used to dray horses than cavalry chargers. He had started life as a brewer's drayman, had stoked the vat in a malthouse, and had by hard work and thrift risen in the world to own a little ship-chandler's shop near the Tower of London.

Okey was a Baptist, an extreme Independent, and in this war he was a volunteer who fought for his beliefs. When Lord Essex flung in his cavalry reserve, John Okey charged valiantly and was soon in the thick of it, at cut and thrust with the royal footguard, the gilded courtiers whom Okey detested.

When Lord Brooke's troop wheeled to charge for a second time, the musketeers of the royal footguard came out in front of their pikemen to check the onset. But they were so shaken by the charge of Brooke's cavalrymen that John Okey saw them 'runne and shrowd themselves within their pikes, not daring to shoot a shot'. The Roundhead pikemen – apprentice lads from the London trained bands – were backing up their cavalry by now, advancing on that wall of Royalist pike-blades to push and chop into them.

Gathered around the Royal Standard, the guards were hewn down one by one. Their colonel, the choleric Lord Lindsey, was mortally wounded. Sir Edmund Verney, Knight Marshal of England, the gentleman who actually held in his grip the scarlet royal banner with its gold lion, was killed where he stood.

The best of the King's levies, a company of obstinate Derbyshire miners, were cut down one by one as the wind blew acrid gunpowder smoke into their faces and they parried pike or sword thrust blindly. Nearly every soldier in the two regiments making this stand for King Charles died fighting.

An experienced and alert royal officer called Sir Charles Lucas had managed by now to rally a couple of hundred stray Cavaliers, and he led them in gallant charge to relieve the pressure on the regiments around the Royal Standard. But his men were too few.

Five troops of Rupert's horse, laden with plunder, came back to the field in the dim light of evening, and to their bewilderment were charged headlong by a single drab-coated but wildly excited troop of Parliamentary horse, including John Okey. 'But they, finding a gap in a hedge,' reported Okey, 'got away.'

Both sides had by now fired off all their powder and were bone-tired. Night was falling. Edgehill, 23 October 1642, had been a confusing battlefield. On both sides men had been rash or cowardly; on both sides men had fought bravely. But neither King Charles's men nor Parliament's had gained the decisive victory, which most Englishmen had secretly hoped might end the war before it had really begun.

A shrewd observer of events said that if either side, on that weary evening, had known the plight the other side was in and had made one final effort, a victory might have been won. But by the time the sun went down, everyone had had a belly-ful of fighting.

The Royalists wearily turned back to climb Edgehill, where the King, clad in armour, dismounted from his horse and held out his arms to his two small sons, James and Charles. The Parliamentary army, badly knocked about, passed that night in the open, on the field of battle amid unburied corpses. The bitter frost of an intensely cold October night is said to have staunched the wounds of many who might otherwise have bled to death.

The stream at the foot of Edgehill had not frozen over.

Wounded men get terribly thirsty. In the starlit night, Round-head and Cavalier alike crept down to the water's edge, to fill bottles for their wounded comrades. As they filled the leather water-bottles from opposite sides of the cold stream, their hands could almost touch.

CHAPTER THREE

London at Bay

I am surprised that any of my ancestors should have permitted such an institution to come into existence
— KING JAMES I, speaking of Parliament

We eat and drink and rise up to play, and this is to live like a gentleman, for what is a gentleman but his pleasure?
— VISCOUNT CONWAY

CAPTAIN Oliver Cromwell, though arriving late on the battlefield of Edgehill with his troop of horse, realized exactly what Parliament needed to win this war. Prince Rupert's cavalry officers might be recklessly brave, but they would never impose the iron discipline that won pitched battles. Given a disciplined cavalry, Parliament would win.

Cromwell, a heavy-set man with sad eyes, had family connections with several leaders of the Puritan cause, but in those early days he was not a leader of the first rank. Indeed, in despair at overthrowing the King's tyrannical counsellors, Cromwell not long before had meditated selling out and emigrating to Massachusetts, to start a new life in America.

Cromwell was not a rich man, either, but a farmer who worked hard raising cattle and growing corn. He had more insight than some of the wealthier Puritan leaders into the feelings of the common people, and he could talk to country people in their own language. Prayer and Bible readings were important in his life, but Cromwell's turbulent and mystic religious emotions were broken up by flashes of clear and profound insight into practical reality.

Oliver Cromwell's political genius lay in penetrating from

the very first battle to the heart of the matter: to overcome the royal power, Parliament must destroy the King's armed force utterly in battle. Control of an army was the key to power. With no armed force at his back, the King of England would be just like any other man. But to win this decisive battle, Parliament must train horsemen able to excel the reckless, high-hearted, courageous Cavaliers. And where were such horsemen to come from?

John Hampden's green-coated infantry regiment of Buckinghamshire volunteers were godly men. They sang psalms on the march, listened to rousing sermons, and disdained all plundering. But of the Parliamentary cavalry when war began, Cromwell wrote to his cousin Hampden 'Your troopers are, most of them, old decayed serving men. Their troopers are gentlemen's sons, younger sons and persons of quality. You must get a man of a spirit that is likely to go as far as a gentleman will go, or else I am sure you will be beaten still.' In other words, put on horseback more men like John Okey, who believed in the righteousness of their cause, and the Cavaliers would never withstand them.

Oliver Cromwell went back to East Anglia, where many small farmers and craftsmen among his neighbours were fervently Puritan, and there he began training cavalry recruits chosen particularly from 'such men as had the fear of God before them, and made some conscience of what they did'.

The battle of Edgehill had decided nothing. Indeed, it had left many Englishmen on both sides sick at heart, and hoping that some way might still be found to escape the bloody trap of war. King Charles, grieving at the loss of so many friends on the battlefield, was one of them. Though he had no intention of giving up his right as King, Charles had begun to show that he lacked ruthlessness.

Hot-blooded Prince Rupert, whose entire life had been war, wanted to ride hard with his cavalry for London, knowing he might well get there before Essex's men had slogged their way home through the autumn mud. Rupert's plan was simple: to ride his horsemen into London and kick Parliament out by force.

But if Rupert's Cavaliers forced their way into London, they would undoubtedly plunder the city down to the bare walls. And what sort of peace would follow that?

So Charles withheld permission for a mad gallop to London – and let his chance go by to win the war with one quick blow. Prince Rupert was in the end allowed to march on London, but only after Londoners had been given time to prepare.

A small elderly man, wearing a mud-stained suit of dark broadcloth, leaned on his mattock and wiped the sweat off his brow. He had a thin intellectual-looking face and was evidently not used to this kind of work. He was a rich Presbyterian merchant called Isaac Pennington and round his neck was a gold chain of office. Isaac Pennington was Lord Mayor of London.

At his side, a plump, decently dressed middle-aged woman, also stained with mud from head to foot, stooped to kirtle up her skirt, then vigorously began to lift shovelfuls of earth out of the ditch in which she stood. She was the Lady Mayoress. The two had come from church and were spending the rest of Sunday digging an entrenchment.

Today from the pulpit, all the Puritan ministers in London, Presbyterian and Independent alike, had urged their congregations to go out and dig trenches to hold back the Cavaliers. The Strand, on the north bank of the river, joined Westminster to the square mile of the City, and in between stretched the suburbs. The plan was to build a ring of forts all the way around and link them by entrenchments. Open streets leading out of the suburbs were to be barricaded, and guns placed to defend them. If the Cavaliers did gallop into London, they would be fought there street by street and house by house.

To get this vast work done in the shortest time, Londoners rich and poor were turning out to help. Members of Parliament and black-clad lawyers from the Inns of Court mustered with pickaxe and spade at seven in the morning in the piazza of Covent Garden. Fishwives marched in procession from Billingsgate, spade over shoulder. One day the entire Company of Vintners, with their wives and servants, took the brunt of the work. Next day, five thousand Shoemakers would march down to the beat of drums, or the Feltmakers, or the City Porters.

Armed pinnaces were brought up the Thames and moored at Westminster to make a last-ditch defence of Parliament, if the Cavaliers did break through. Twenty thousand volunteers at any one time, including women and children, were at work on the fortifications with pick and shovel and they got no pay except their food. All were united in the common desire that London should not become a battlefield.

But if Prince Rupert did manage to break into London, he was certain to find many friends there. In their hearts, many Londoners were for King Charles. The Royalists in London, as the King's army came closer, were raising their heads and spreading discontent at every chance.

For example, Isaac Pennington had called upon the people of London to give up their silver tankards to the war chest. As Lord Mayor, he had also made people pay two shillings for a pass to leave London – partly as a tax, but partly as a precaution against treachery.

The tax was irksome and unpopular, and in Royalist taverns they were already singing this ditty against the Puritan Lord Mayor:

Farewell little Isaac, with hey, with hey,
Farewell little Isaac, with hoe,
    Thou has made us all, like Asses,
    Part with our plate, and drink in Glasses
    Whilst thou growest rich with two shilling passes,
With hey, trolly lolly loe.

On 29 October 1642, the House of Lords proposed to open
negotiations for peace. The King announced himself as willing to make some concessions to the 'tender consciences' of
all those, Presbyterians and Independents alike, who disliked
using an Anglican prayer-book service in church. Parliament
for their own part declared themselves ready to welcome King
Charles back to Westminster 'without his bad advisers'.

But the real issue in the conflict was who should rule, who
should have the power to tax and to raise armies, King or
Parliament? On this main point Charles offered no concessions, and John Pym, the political leader of those determined to crush King Charles, knew he was never likely to.
The war would go on.

In the early morning of 12 November 1642, a heavy mist rose
from the River Thames, obscuring the streets of the little
market town of Brentford, which guarded the western approaches to London. Brentford was garrisoned for Parliament
with two regiments – Denzil Holles's red-coated, crop-haired
apprentice lads, who had fought so bravely at Edgehill, and
an infantry regiment now commanded by Lord Brooke.

That morning when dressing, Prince Rupert put on, for
once, not his usual spectacular attire, but a drab grey cloak,
which made him almost invisible in the thick mist. At about
dawn, he led a roaring attack, at the head of the King's Welsh
infantry, on the garrison at Brentford. Meanwhile, his
Cavaliers reined in outside the little town and awaited their

moment. 'All butchers and dyers!' they remarked contemptuously of the amateur soldiers holding Brentford, who blocked their way to London.

Denzil Holles's red-uniformed young men stood their ground behind improvised barricades of wagons and furniture and fought the wild Welshmen with pike and musket. But Lord Brooke's men ran in panic, some of them trying to escape with their lives by swimming the ice-cold Thames.

All turned their backs except one man, a twenty-seven-year-old captain called John Lilburne. Left alone in the confusion, he seized the regimental colours and managed to defend them single-handed. He was overwhelmed at last while trying to rally a handful of his comrades, and made prisoner.

Several hundred of Parliament's young soldiers, mostly in the scarlet of Holles's regiment, lay dead in the misty streets of Brentford by the time John Hampden came up with his psalm-singing greencoats to act as rearguard and cover the retreat of the survivors. Prince Rupert had taken five hundred other prisoners, as well as Captain Lilburne, and fifteen guns.

Even before his single-handed fight that day at Brentford, John Lilburne, charming, witty, but a young man of burning sincerity and compelling eloquence, had been a hero to the London apprentice lads. Six years earlier, when he was an apprentice like themselves, John Lilburne had defied the King's court of the Star Chamber. The bishops had been trying to prevent the circulation of books of religious polemic printed abroad by English printers. But young Lilburne had stood up boldly for the freedom of the press – and had been condemned for it to be whipped all the way across London from Fleet Street to Palace Yard. Ever since then 'Freeborn John' had been idolized by the young men in the City who loved liberty, and now he was a prisoner in the hands of his enemies.

*

Rupert signalled the Cavaliers to ride up and put the little town of Brentford to the sack. Horsemen came clattering in, and Brentford endured a long afternoon of wild destruction. All the valuables were carried off, and the Royalist troopers, in a destructive mood, then began to slit open feather beds with their swords and to set thatched roofs afire. The town echoed with the screams of molested women.

Soon the tale of the plundering of Brentford got back to London, and John Pym's cronies went out of their way to exaggerate the horrors. Many Londoners who had been hoping for peace now hardened their hearts. At all costs, these ferocious plundering Cavaliers must be kept out of London.

On 13 November, King Charles's advancing army paused. The armed might of all London confronted them at Turnham Green, a village on the north bank of the Thames, which had been selected by Parliamentarian Philip Skippon as the right place to make a stand, because the fenced-in vegetable gardens there would hamper the charge of cavalry.

The King's generals reined in half a mile away, out of the range of musket shot, and there before them, marshalled for battle, was such an enemy army as they had never expected to see, much less wanted to attack.

Behind the banners at Turnham Green were rallied the horse and foot of the London trained bands, now 16,000 strong. Flanking them were the City's new regiments of volunteers. Thousands of survivors from Lord Essex's army at Edgehill had also reached London and had taken their place in its organized defence, bringing the total of armed and trained men confronting King Charles amid the peaceful vegetable gardens of Turnham Green to 24,000.

The Cavaliers had expected to gallop merrily into London, as they had into Brentford. At the sight of that mass of armed citizens, their hearts sank.

Philip Skippon, the staunch veteran of the Dutch wars, rose in his stirrups at the head of his still and silent army of Londoners and, turning to face them, spoke at the top of his old-soldier's voice.

'Come, my boys, my brave boys – let us pray heartily and fight heartily. I will run the same fortunes and hazards with you. Remember the cause is for God, and for the defence of yourselves, your wives and children.'

From the ranks came a fervent 'Amen!'

When the Earl of Essex arrived, smoking a long clay pipe as usual, the soldiers who had served under him at Edgehill merrily threw their caps in the air, shouting 'Hey for old Robin!'

Halted out of range of musket shot after their hungry march halfway across England, the men in the ranks of the King's army saw in the distance a procession of a hundred loaded carts, which had rumbled out from London. They were driven by women. Today was Sunday, and the citizens' wives were sending thousands of good hot dinners, with meat and ale and pudding, to their men.

King Charles at that moment had a choice. Either he could submit to Parliament's will and satisfy himself with being a national figurehead, with no authoritative powers, or else he must push those 24,000 determined Londoners out of the way. To his way of thinking, both choices were impossible.

After showing their exasperation by firing off a few cannon shots, the King and Prince Rupert turned their army around and retreated, foiled, towards the royal headquarters at Christ Church, Oxford.

There in Oxford, the King in a moment of vindictiveness put his old enemy, John Lilburne, on trial for treason, though Lilburne, as a serving officer, should have been regarded as a prisoner of war. Lilburne was condemned to death, and only wily old John Pym's prompt threat to hang, draw and quarter some of the important Royalists who were prisoner in the hands of Parliament saved Lilburne's neck.

King Charles struck a silver medal at Oxford to reward acts of gallantry, and made plans for the next year's campaign. The confrontation at Turnham Green had given Londoners breathing space. But all over the north and west of England the King's friends were preparing. By the spring, when Charles planned to have 40,000 men in the field, his chance would come.

John Pym, the Puritans' cleverest political leader, saw with starker clarity than most the real danger. Since in the short run the King's friends could undoubtedly bring a greater military force to bear than Parliament was likely to raise and train, they still might win a decisive battle. Where could Parliament turn for help?

Charles was also King of Scotland, but most of the Scots in the Lowlands were Presbyterians and had no special love for him. Suppose the Scots could be persuaded to invade England with an army that would fight for Parliament's cause? Slowly, patiently, John Pym began intriguing to find out what the price might be for the Scots to send an army against their own King.

In Oxford that winter there were jokes. For instance, Boy, Prince Rupert's white poodle, was promoted to Major General. But London had been a gloomy place since the war began. The Puritans closed the theatres, on the excuse that plays were 'spectacles of pleasure too commonly expressing lascivious mirth and levity'. In the suburbs the poorer citizens shivered with cold, because Newcastle, the port that in normal times sent 'seacoal' to London, was occupied by a royal army, and the King was trying to buy arms by selling the coal overseas.

But at least the bishops' censorship of the press was a thing of the past. Pamphlets and newsletters and eventually the first real English newspapers poured out from the printing presses. To a serious-minded man, London was intellectually stimulating. But it was not much fun.

The Royalists in Oxford decided to turn this new freedom of the press to their own advantage. They decided to make Londoners laugh at the Puritans. From January 1643 onwards, they published a witty and mocking newspaper called *Mercurius Aulicus*, which soon all London was itching to read on the sly. *Mercurius Aulicus* sold for a penny, and it was full of songs and ballads and spicy news, not to mention derisive jokes about such crude puritanical actions as cutting down maypoles and banning mince pies.

Getting the paper from Oxford to its readers in London was not easy. Bundles would be dropped under hedges well outside Oxford by Prince Rupert's cavalry pickets. They were picked up by women devoted to the royal cause, who often travelled the roads dressed as beggars and smuggled the printed sheets into London under their skirts. Soon the demand for *Mercurius Aulicus* was so great that copies marked at a penny were changing hands at eighteen pence. And when the Londoners laughed, their laughter served King Charles.

CHAPTER FOUR

Run like Wildfire

The necessitous people of the whole kingdom will presently rise in mighty numbers. If this unruly sort have once cast the rider, it will run like wildfire in example through all the counties of England – From a secret correspondence between Captain John Hotham, son of the Parliamentary governor of Hull, and the Earl of Newcastle, royal commander in the north.

AFTER his setback at Turnham Green, the King's new plan was to crush London as in a giant nut-cracker. The army of the north, led and paid for by William Cavendish, the immensely rich Earl of Newcastle, would act as one jaw of the nut-cracker. The other jaw would be the army of the west, centred around a valiant little band of Cornishmen, led by Sir Ralph Hopton.

Sir Ralph was a good-hearted gentleman, and a Royalist to his fingertips. He had fought in Bohemia for Prince Rupert's mother, Queen Elizabeth. Once war broke out, King Charles sent him into the far west of England, and there Sir Ralph had managed to raise a royal army almost from nothing.

The Cornish gentry came in on horseback as volunteer cavalry, and the tin miners of Cornwall – enough to form five infantry regiments – were eager to serve their King. The Cornish fishermen put to sea as royal privateers. But where were the weapons to come from and how were the men to be paid?

Luck played into Sir Ralph Hopton's hands. In stormy weather in the English Channel, his privateers came up with a fleet of forty sail and chivvied them ashore under the guns of Pendennis Castle, a Royalist stronghold. They proved to be Parliament ships, loaded with weapons and money. Sir Ralph was able not only to equip, but even to pay his little army, and to take them on the first step of their long march towards London.

On 19 January 1643, Sir Ralph fought a small-scale pitched battle at Braddock Down with a Parliamentary force out of Plymouth. The pluck of his Cornish infantry won the day. Hopton took 1,250 Roundheads prisoner, and captured five guns. His little army now even had artillery.

But the Roundhead port of Plymouth, kept going by ships of the Parliamentary navy, was too strong for Sir Ralph Hopton's men to capture. And the further his Cornishmen marched towards London, the more aware they became of having Roundheads at their back, right there in Plymouth, and near enough to Cornwall to raid their unprotected homes.

Lord Newcastle, who had raised 2,000 horse and 6,000 foot for King Charles in the north, was fifty years old, and very rich. He was a splendid fencer, one of the best horsemen in Europe, and personally very brave, but he had no talent whatever as a general, and well knew it. He left the humdrum business of running his army to a mercenary soldier called James King, who had fought in Germany and had recently been ennobled as Lord Eythin.

Lord Newcastle wore his hair long, and he was reputed by his enemies to spend an hour every day combing it. He travelled to battle in a luxurious coach pulled by six well-matched horses and furnished with musical instruments and a select library.

Lord Newcastle's secret ambition was to become famous as a poet. He paid Shirley and Dryden generously to polish his verses and appointed another poet, Sir William Davenant, as his general of artillery. In battle, Lord Newcastle liked best to mount his charger and fight in the ranks, like any other Cavalier.

The best of Newcastle's infantry were men from the Border – tough men, whose ancestors had carried on an irregular cattle-raiding warfare with the Scots for generations. Their uniforms had been made in a hurry, of undyed cloth, so they cheerfully accepted the nickname of Whitecoats and promised Lord Newcastle that at the first opportunity they would dye the white cloth red with enemy blood.

In November 1642, shortly before Sir Ralph Hopton began coming up from the west, Lord Newcastle took the first step on his march towards London. He occupied the cathedral city of York without much difficulty, but then his advance slowed down. On his left flank was the fortified port of Hull, supplied by the Parliamentary navy, which threatened his lines of communication, much as Plymouth threatened Hopton's. On his right, he was harassed by a small but intrepid force of Roundhead cavalry, raised in Yorkshire by Sir Thomas Fairfax and his father.

Black Tom Fairfax, with his large dark eyes and prominent beaklike nose, was something of a dandy, too, and no less fond than Lord Newcastle of poetry, music, and animals. He had let his raven locks grow long and he dressed with elegance. Young Fairfax might easily have passed for a Cavalier.

The poor Yorkshire weavers, now that the war had reached their county, could scarcely make a living. Sir Thomas Fairfax was a generous-hearted man who tried to help them; they would follow Black Tom anywhere, because he identified his fate with theirs. He led his little force of amateur cavalry against Lord Newcastle's army with a fox-hunter's eye for landscape and the audacity of a born general.

*

Lord Newcastle had captured York, but dare he risk marching further south? The presence of Fairfax and his bold horsemen somewhere up on the moors was worrying. Newcastle paused, to train recruits and wait for spring weather, and the royal advance on London from the north slowed down to a standstill.

On 18 December 1642, Lord Newcastle ordered Sir William Savile to go into the West Riding, with one thousand men, and capture the little Puritan clothing town of Bradford.

There were no Roundhead troops in Bradford, and no defences, but the weavers there decided to make a fight of it. A few had muskets but most took 'scythes, long poles, spits, clubs and suchlike rustic weapons' and they bravely held back Savile and his large Royalist force until the Roundheads in Halifax could march over the moors to their aid.

'We had never a gentleman in the parish to command us,' wrote a Bradford man proudly, adding 'The courage in our army astonished the enemy, who said that no fifty men, unless they were mad or drunk, would have pursued a thousand.'

Next day Sir Thomas Fairfax and his father trotted down from the moors into Bradford with three troops of cavalry and 120 dragoons – four hundred horsemen in all. Finding the men of Bradford and Halifax too much for him, Sir William Savile had retreated eastward to the market town of Leeds, where the road to London crossed a bridge over the River Aire.

Leeds in those days had one long wide street, Briggate, where the cloth market was held. At the lower end of Briggate, the bridge crossed the Aire, and across the top end, at right angles, ran another main street, the Headrow. Entrenchments had been dug from the Headrow down to the river, enclosing the town inside a fortified square. These trenches were lined by Sir William Savile's musketeers. More earthworks defended Briggate, and two nine-pounder cannon commanded the bridge.

Sir Thomas Fairfax sent Captain Mildmay along the south bank of the River Aire with thirty musketeers, a company of his dragoons, and a thousand 'clubmen' – unarmed Puritan Yorkshiremen, who took up any improvised weapon they could lay their hands on. Young Fairfax led the rest of his mounted force along the north bank of the Aire to Woodhouse Moor, overlooking the Headrow. By now, Sir William Savile was holding Leeds with fifteen hundred well-armed footsoldiers and five troops of horse.

The attack on the bridge over the Aire and on the trenches defending it began at two in the afternoon. The thousand clubmen armed with scythes and kitchen spits and cudgels, and led by Jonathan Scholfield, a minister from Halifax, marched up to the very mouths of the cannon, singing the sixty-eighth Psalm: '*Let God arise, and His enemies will be scattered.*' They seized upon the two threatening nine-pounders almost with their bare hands.

Black Tom's battlecry was 'Emanuel'. Yelling 'Emanuel!' the fearless Yorkshiremen broke across the bridge and into the Cavalier trenches. They had turned the two nine-pounder guns around and were firing them on the foe, driving the Royalists up Briggate, when from Headrow came more shouts of 'Emanuel!' Black Tom Fairfax came in sight, conspicuous on a white horse, his long hair streaming behind him. He had led his handful of cavalry in a tremendous charge down from Woodhouse Moor to the Headrow. The Cavaliers were crushed between two fires.

By four that afternoon the Yorkshire Puritans had taken possession of Leeds, together with 460 prisoners, 14 precious barrels of gunpowder, and many muskets. Black Tom's father, Lord Fairfax, reporting the victory to Parliament,

wrote proudly 'My son, upon the taking of Leeds, though he
entered it by force, yet he restrained his army from pillaging.'

Sir Thomas Fairfax detested plunder. He was never a man
who understood much about politics, or cared much, either.
But he was convinced from the start that Parliament could
win this war only by earning the help of the common people,
the ones who suffered most.

Lord Newcastle realized that before advancing on London,
he must first crush Fairfax and his men, but he took his time
about it. Six months later, on 30 June 1643, Lord Newcastle
arrived on Adwalton Moor, overlooking Bradford, with an
army ten thousand strong, including two huge demi-cannon
weighing five tons apiece, named Gog and Magog, each towed
by twenty horses.

By this time the poor weavers of the West Riding of
Yorkshire were in dire distress. The harvest had been bad,
the cloth trade was at a standstill, and there were no stocks
of food. Bradford was not much more than a large village protected by a few entrenchments, and certainly could not withstand an enemy with siege guns. The battle must be fought
on the moor.

The Fairfaxes, father and son, came out of Bradford at
seven of that midsummer morning with fewer than four thousand men behind them, to confront Newcastle's ten thousand.

Young Sir Thomas Fairfax, commanding the Puritan
army's right wing, lined a big hedged field in front of him
with a thousand musketeers, including his dismounted dragoons. By firing from cover they would break the impact of
Newcastle's cavalry charges.

Black Tom then led his own little cavalry force in a reckless charge against the mass of the royal army. He was driven
back, but, as he had hoped, he provoked a countercharge by
a much larger brigade of Cavaliers. This enemy attack was

broken up by the fire of musketeers in ambush behind their
hedges, giving Black Tom yet another chance to lead his fearless handful of troopers in a headlong onslaught against the
enemy. Out on that flank, the whole day went by in this kind
of desperate charge and countercharge, which began to wear
the Cavaliers down.

Lord Newcastle was actually wondering whether it might
not be prudent to withdraw his men from the field when an
attack on the flank furthest from Black Tom by Royalist pikemen led by Colonel Kirton, 'a wild and desperate man', drove
the Roundhead troops on that side of the field back in disorder.

The outnumbered Puritan line was broken, and the centre
collapsed soon after, the Roundheads fleeing pell mell. This
left Sir Thomas Fairfax's devoted handful of cavalry and
musketeers alone on the field, a target for all the Royalist
guns. Newcastle's entire army of ten thousand converged on
and overwhelmed them.

Though Black Tom's men were almost surrounded, and
were by now outnumbered eight to one, he kept them well in
hand, and they managed to cut their way through to the
Halifax road. Fairfax paused there to collect the survivors of
the defeat of Adwalton Moor, and he led them in a spirited
fighting retreat through hostile country to the Parliamentary
port of Hull. He arrived in Hull with 1,500 footsoldiers and
700 horse – a valuable reinforcement to the city's defences.

In a besieged city, horses eat up food badly needed by
humans, and are usually not much use in the fighting. So Sir
Thomas Fairfax led his cavalry chargers out of Hull and
across the Humber estuary, to join the remarkable cavalry
that Colonel Cromwell had been training for the Eastern
Association, the counties of East Anglia which had come together in the Puritan cause.

Plain-featured, downright Lady Fairfax, who had been

taken prisoner on the retreat and set free again by Lord Newcastle as an act of gallantry, decided that her rightful place
was with her husband's Yorkshiremen in besieged Hull. On
parting from Sir Thomas she gave him a locket to wear round
his neck in battle, engraved with the words *Rather die than
truth deny.*

Sir Thomas Fairfax and Oliver Cromwell, meeting for the
first time, instantly liked and trusted one another, though in
temperament they differed greatly.

Fairfax was young, gentle, scholarly, and courteous. He
was more moderate in his behaviour than most Presbyterians,
though his wife, who always egged him on, was a perfervid
believer. Cromwell was a blunt, middle-aged, outspoken countryman with no airs and graces, but his men trusted him, and
in leading an army of amateur soldiers to victory that was
what essentially mattered.

Cromwell was an Independent, and to begin with, before he
got a taste for power, he fought because he believed that only
a complete victory over King Charles would bring religious
freedom.

Already, Cromwell had been testing out his new cavalry
against Newcastle's Cavaliers along the northerly borders of
East Anglia. Of the men he was training to fight, Cromwell
had declared frankly 'I would rather have a plain, russet-
coated captain that knows what he fights for and loves what
he knows, than that which you call a gentleman and is
nothing else.' They were certainly plain men, mostly yeoman
farmers' sons, and, like Fairfax's bluff Yorkshiremen, they
had already been discovering for themselves that gentlemen
on horseback, the Cavaliers, were not invincible.

CHAPTER FIVE

Apprentices to Gloucester

All were Englishmen, and pity it was that such courage
should be spent in blood of each other –
BULSTRODE WHITELOCK, after the first battle of Newbury

There were very few of the common people that cared
much for either of the causes, but would have taken any side
for pay or plunder   – THOMAS HOBBES

ON a chill February morning in 1643, a handsome, lively
woman with big eyes and dark ringlets sat in an open boat
that was plunging through chill grey waves towards a shore
blurred by snowflakes. The Queen was coming back to
England.

The ladies-in-waiting crowded around Henrietta Maria in
the pitching boat; their faces had turned ominously green.
The seamen muttered Dutch curses as they tugged at their
oars. But the Queen smiled and encouraged them all. She
feared nothing.

As a French princess, and very self-conscious about her
gawkiness, Henrietta Maria had been married to King
Charles when she was only sixteen. In the strange English
court she had clung to her religion, and given all the protection she could to the English Roman Catholics, though she
failed to convert her husband to Catholicism, or her nephew
Prince Rupert. But Henrietta had managed to stop the persecution of English Catholics, and for this reason she was a
woman the Puritans hated.

Cavalry officers from Lord Newcastle's army were waiting
anxiously on the shore. They reached out eager hands to

Cavalry Exercise: the trooper mounts and prepares to load his pistol (National Army Museum)

help the Queen and her ladies up the slippery stairs of Bridlington quay. The Queen, with her pet spaniel Mitte in the crook of her arm, stood on the cobblestones shaking the snow out of her hair and graciously thanking her helpers.

Offshore, tossing on the grey waves, were six merchantmen convoyed by seven Dutch men-of-war. The Queen had managed to pawn the Crown Jewels in Holland for £180,000, and in those ships she was bringing back with her enough weapons to fill 140 wagons, and to equip a small army.

However, the danger was not yet over.

Five Parliamentary ships had arrived, commanded by Lord Warwick's Vice-Admiral, William Batten. Though they kept at a prudent distance from those seven Dutch men-of-war, their job was to stop the Queen's convoy from getting through. But by now the Queen's ammunition ships had come close inshore. While Henrietta Maria plodded through the snow to inspect her cavalry escort, seamen began briskly unloading the precious munitions and stacking them on the quay.

In his flagship, the 40-gun *Rainbow*, Vice-Admiral Batten bided his time. After dusk, he sent a small rowing boat ashore. The coxswain asked a passer-by to point out to him the cottage where the Queen of England lay sleeping. At five

Cavalry Exercise: the trooper charges his pistol with powder
(*National Army Museum*)

the next morning, in the first light of a winter's day, Captain
Batten's flotilla opened fire with a hundred guns. Their target
was not the moored ammunition ships, or the weapons and
gunpowder piled along the quay. His gunners had been
ordered to concentrate their fire upon one target alone – the
cottage.

Henrietta Maria and her ladies tumbled downstairs and ran
in the bitter cold to the cover of a snowfilled ditch. But the
Queen's little spaniel Mitte had been left behind, and Henrietta Maria ran alone through the whizzing cannonballs to
rescue the dog. 'The balls were surging round us in fine style,'
she wrote to King Charles afterwards, 'and a sergeant was
killed, twenty paces from me.'

Batten's attempt to murder the Queen by cannon fire did
not last long. The Dutch admiral, Maartin Tromp, sailed his
seven warships across Bridlington Bay to block off the shore,
and ran out their guns. Vice-Admiral Batten took the hint.
His guns fell silent.

Henrietta Maria and her train of loaded wagons went off
first to York, to help equip Lord Newcastle's army, then jour-
neyed southwards to join the King. The Queen was enter-
tained at Stratford-upon-Avon by Shakespeare's grand-
daughter, and the next day she met Charles, after seventeen

Cavalry Exercise: the trooper rams the bullet into his pistol
(National Army Museum)

months of separation. Some counsellors on the King's side
had begun by now to murmur about the advantages of a
negotiated peace. But never Henrietta Maria.

Cavaliers based at Oxford were keeping the Earl of Essex
and his army busy with raids up the Thames valley and over
the Chiltern Hills to the very outskirts of London. So to hold
back the royal army, advancing gradually from the west of
England, Parliament formed a second Roundhead army and
gave command to Sir William Waller, a rich landowning
Member of Parliament who had been a soldier in the continental wars. Waller was said to be clever at defensive warfare, and he succeeded, to begin with, in hampering Cavalier
Sir Ralph Hopton and his men. But his final clash with them,
at Roundway Down near Devizes, on 13 July 1643, was the
greatest Cavalier victory so far in the war.

Half Sir William Waller's cavalry was led by Sir Arthur
Haselrig, another of the Five Members. Haselrig had a notion
of his own about the best way to beat the King's cavalry.
Cromwell wanted to put a better type of man on horseback,
but Haselrig advocated a different type of equipment – complete armour, inside which a Roundhead trooper would

Cavalry Exercise: the trooper cocks his pistol and – after obeying twenty successive orders – is at last ready to fire (National Army Museum)

feel safe. He trained and led a force of cuirassiers – cavalry-men dressed from head to foot in armour and mounted on heavy carthorses.

The five hundred cuirassiers commanded by Haselrig in Sir William Waller's army were nicknamed the Lobsters. Among them was a man who had been used to handling big dray horses in peacetime, and who as a cavalryman had been in continual action since the first battle of the war – John Okey, the Baptist ship's chandler, now promoted to major.

Sir Ralph Hopton was pushing on to join forces with the King at Oxford. He and his Cornishmen had already reached the small, unfortified town of Devizes, forty-five miles from the royal headquarters, but they were desperately short of ammunition because Haselrig and his Lobsters had managed to stop a convoy of powder and shot.

To block Hopton's way, Sir William Waller posted his army on a big chalk hill called Roundway Down, which over-looked Devizes. To command the little town, he set up a battery of guns there. Waller intended that Hopton should go no further, but he did not move his men downhill fast enough to ring Devizes from all sides.

Before Waller could blockade Devizes, Sir Ralph Hopton ordered his cavalry to break out and ride hard for the royal headquarters in Oxford. They left on the gallop just as midnight struck, and the Lobsters were not fast enough to catch them. For three days, Sir Ralph and his infantry sat it out in Devizes, under bombardment day and night from the enemy guns on Roundway Down, and so short of ammunition that to make bullets they were obliged to melt down lead guttering from the roofs.

Many Cavaliers had just left Oxford to escort home Henrietta Maria's great convoy of munitions. Only 1,800 horsemen could be spared. They were led by Sir Harry Wilmot, a recklessly gay courtier before the war, and a dashing cavalry leader ever since. Sir Ralph Hopton was by now almost blind from a wound, and cooped up in Devizes with him were 3,000 foot. Sir William Waller's army, poised threateningly above him on Roundway Down, numbered 4,500, mostly cavalry, but it also included 2,000 foot and those eight field guns that were pounding Devizes day and night.

As Harry Wilmot and his Oxford Cavaliers approached at the gallop over the grassy downs, they made the agreed signal – two cannon shots – to warn Hopton's infantry in Devizes. But the Royalists trapped inside the town doubted at first that help could arrive so fast. Suppose one of their own side had been taken prisoner, and the enemy had learned the signal? Those two cannon shots might be a trick to lure them out.

While the infantrymen in Devizes were making up their minds, Harry Wilmot up on Roundway Down ordered his own horsemen into three brigades to give battle. Since Hopton's infantry was taking its time about marching out of Devizes to join him, Harry Wilmot decided to attack Waller's army, though so much larger than his own, with only his cavalry. The decision was typically Cavalier – recklessly irregular, according to the strict laws of war, but so well timed and so dashing that it astounded the enemy.

The Cavalier brigade on Harry Wilmot's left trotted forward in an extended line, three men deep, to encounter Haselrig's Lobsters. Now for these men on heavy horses came the testing time. The Cavaliers had been given strict orders to hold their fire until the Lobsters were at point-blank range, since a bullet fired from any distance would probably bounce off their helmets and suits of armour.

Haselrig had drawn up his cuirassiers compactly in six lines, slow to move, but heavy to shift. They felt safe inside their heavy armour, but they were slow, clumsy, and inert. What wins a cavalry action is dash – the offensive spirit. This the Lobsters sorely lacked.

As Wilmot's men trotted closer, the Lobsters fired off their carbines from the saddle. The advancing Cavaliers broke from a canter into a gallop. Spurring their heavy chargers from a shuffling walk to a slow trot, the Lobsters gave the Royalist horsemen a volley from their pistols.

But it took more than pistol shots to check a charge of Cavaliers, and when it came to hand-to-hand fighting against a brave and dexterous antagonist, a heavily armoured Lobster was trapped. The long line of Cavaliers, distinctive in their buffcoats, swung around the six lines of Lobsters to outflank and overlap them, enfolding them from sight.

The men in gleaming armour astride their heavy horses could clearly be seen giving ground, and the sight unnerved the other Roundheads. Soon Sir Arthur Haselrig and his men had had enough and were thudding away from the battle on their clumsy steeds, Sir Arthur himself in the lead.

Captain Richard Atkyns, a Cavalier who later wrote about the battle, picked out Sir Arthur Haselrig as his prey, and chased after him. Atkyns rode alongside Haselrig and fired his pistol at point-blank range. The slug was deflected by the armour, and Atkyns's hacking blows with the sword bounced off Sir Arthur's helmet and cuirass. The Lobsters' commander got away with a whole skin.

But now the rest of the Roundhead cavalry, struck hard by the charge of Wilmot's second and third brigades, had begun to turn their backs and follow the Lobsters in their rumbling flight off the field of battle.

The triumphant Cavaliers, having 'swept their whole body of horse out of the field', chased the Roundheads three miles across the turf of Roundway Down to a breakneck descent on the far side. Dozens of Roundhead cavalrymen one after another fell down headlong to their death.

The victorious Cavaliers nicknamed the battle of Roundway Down 'Runaway Down'. Six hundred Roundheads were killed, eight hundred taken prisoner, and Waller's army was made ineffective. Hopton's men reached Oxford just as the Queen's big convoy of arms and ammunition came in. King Charles's grand strategy, a pincer attack on London, was one big step closer.

Prince Rupert united his forces with Sir Ralph Hopton's, and together they turned and marched westward to capture Bristol, the second port in the kingdom. At sea, thanks to the leadership of the piratical Earl of Warwick, the Parliamentarians had so far had it nearly all their own way. King Charles badly needed a good port and an effective naval force.

The shipping in the port of Bristol could serve as the nucleus of a fleet, and the city itself, being five miles up a river, could be surrounded with soldiers and put to the assault on all sides, unlike a port on the coast, like Plymouth or Hull, which Warwick's navy could succour.

The Roundheads had the wealth and resources of London at their back, so they could manufacture arms. They controlled the part of England that then was economically most developed. But King Charles, for the most part, had to arm his men with weapons bought abroad. He desperately needed a port under his own control.

On 23 July 1643, Prince Rupert and his dragoon commander, the redoubtable Colonel Henry Washington, rode together across Durdham Down, just outside Bristol, and reined in at Clifton Church. There, a few hundred yards off, they could trace the long defensive earth wall, interrupted by forts and strong points, that had been built up and down hills to encircle Bristol. Roundhead artillerymen in the fort noticed their gay clothes and, guessing they were Cavaliers, promptly opened fire.

From the spire of Clifton Church, Rupert and Washington carefully observed the fortified city below – a central huddle of spires and towers and a gleaming fork of river water, thick with ships' masts. The wall around Bristol was five miles long and would need many soldiers to defend it.

Yet to guard this long perimeter, Colonel Fiennes, the Parliamentary governor, had been left with only 300 horse and 1,500 foot, because Sir William Waller had drawn heavily on Bristol's garrison for reinforcements before his army was destroyed at Roundway Down. One royal victory was leading straight to another.

Among the citizens of Bristol were many Puritans, who were untrained but willing to fight courageously for their homes and their beliefs. But many others were secretly Royalist, and the richest among them had put their plate and coin aboard eight armed ships moored out in the river, ready to flee or surrender depending on how the tide of battle flowed.

Prince Rupert named 26 July as the day for storming the walls of Bristol. Each King's man was to wear a sprig of green and go into battle without a neckcloth, bare-throated. The strongest point in the city's defence was Prior's Hill Fort, and here the Cavaliers made their greatest effort. Captain Fawcett tried to blow in the gate with a powder bag – a dangerous dodge. The bag exploded, but the gate stood.

Fighting then began outside the fort, hand to hand. A ditch six feet wide served as a moat, and soon it was filled to the top with Royalist dead. An attack on nearby Windmill Hill Fort had also failed, and Prince Rupert, as he rallied some of his disheartened soldiers for a second try, had his horse shot from under him.

Colonel Harry Washington, Prince Rupert's dragoon commander, was a particularly observant man, and he noticed that the stretch of wall between Windmill Hill Fort and Brandon Hill Fort had been badly designed. Near the earth wall was a patch of 'dead ground' safe from the fire of the city's defenders.

At the head of his dismounted dragoons, hurling grenades over the wall as he ran, Washington ran full tilt towards this safe patch through a murderously hot crossfire. Then, huddling together under the mud wall in the shelter of the dead ground, Washington and his dragoons wrenched open a breach with a sergeant's halberd and their own bare hands.

Through this narrow breach, with a blazing firepike held high, galloped Lieutenant-Colonel Littleton. To cries of 'Wildfire!' the alarmed Roundheads along the earthwork fled. Soon three hundred Cavaliers had leaped their mounts over that stretch of wall or charged them straight through the breach and were making helter skelter for Bristol's inner defences, her old medieval city wall.

At the Frome Gate in the inner wall, an obstinate two-hour defence was made by soldier and citizen alike. The Cavaliers at last broke through, but just inside the city wall they were held up by yet another obstacle. Two hundred Bristol housewives, working amid smoke and shot, had raised up a barricade of earth and woolsacks for a third line of defence. Desperate fighting was still going on around those woolsacks when Colonel Fiennes, the Puritan governor of Bristol, acknowledged defeat and surrendered the city.

Prince Rupert's terms of surrender were generous. Officers were allowed to keep their arms, and all ranks were granted the right to march out of the city gates 'with bag and baggage'. Many of the Cavaliers chose to jeer and mock as their defeated Roundhead enemy marched away. In the nasal tones of Puritan preachers, they loudly inquired, 'And where wert Thou at Runaway Hill, O Lord? And where art Thou today?'

At last the sight of the defeated enemy soldiers actually being allowed to carry off their personal property became too much for Royalist discipline. A mob of King's men surged forward, broke into the marching Roundhead ranks, and stripped them bare.

This made Prince Rupert immensely angry. Spurring his horse into the midst of his own men, he drew his sword and began laying about him left and right with the flat of the blade. Rupert had given his word, as a soldier and a gentleman, on the terms of surrender, and now these plunderers were dishonouring him.

Now the great port of Bristol – the second city of the kingdom – was in King Charles's hands once more, and there remained only one Roundhead strongpoint hampering a Royalist advance on London from the west. The cathedral city of Gloucester, at the crossing of the River Severn from Wales into England, was held for the Roundheads by young Colonel Massey. To leave Puritan Gloucester blocking the King's line of communication with Royalist Wales would be folly. And after Gloucester would come London.

Of the Five Members – the five Puritan Members of Parliament, most of them rich, whose escape from King Charles

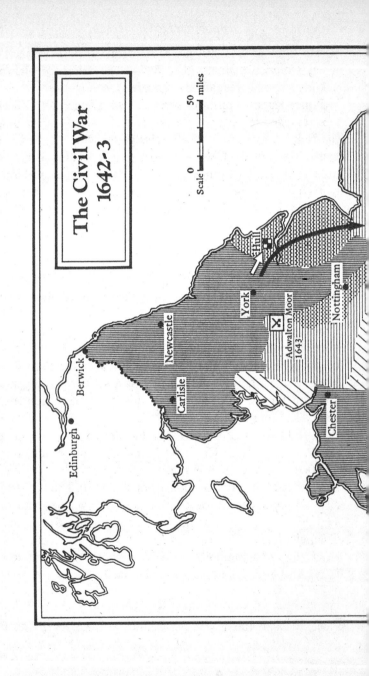

**The Civil War
1642-3**

Scale

0   50 miles

Edinburgh

Berwick

Carlisle

Newcastle

York

Hull

Adwalton Moor
1643

Nottingham

Chester

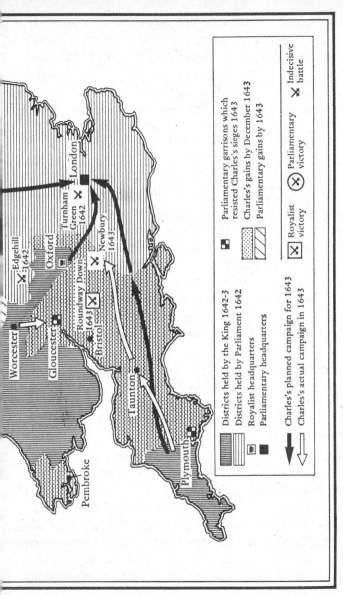

In 1642 Londoners at Turnham Green kept the King's Army out of his capital city – the largest city in the land and a Parliamentary stronghold. So King Charles adopted a pincer strategy – armies from the North and West would move on London like the jaws of a nut-cracker closing.

had signalled the outbreak of war – Sir Arthur Haselrig, after his fiasco at Roundway Down, was discredited; John Hampden had been killed in a skirmish at the head of his men; John Pym, the cleverest political leader among them and the least religious, was dying of an agonizing disease; and Denzil Holles, who never recovered from the moral shock of seeing his scarlet-clad young volunteers cut up at Edgehill and Brentford, was now heading the Peace Party in the House of Commons.

Like other rich men who had begun by thinking that war on the King was necessary, Denzil Holles was by now deeply unhappy about the way the Civil War was going. King Charles's restrictions and monopolies might at times have been very irksome, especially to ambitious men who wanted to make money, but royal authority gave all forms of property equal protection, and under King Charles's paternal rule, the poor had known their place. The war was putting arms into poor men's hands and ideas into their heads. England was being stirred up and would never be the same again.

In London, the Puritans had clumsily managed to raise a riot among their own best volunteer soldiers, the young apprentices. By now many Members of Parliament of moderate opinion had already gone to Oxford to join the King. This left the Presbyterians in a large majority in Parliament. After the theatres had been closed, they set up a Parliamentary Committee under Sir Robert Harley to destroy 'all superstitious or idolatrous monuments'.

Most Puritans believed that every word of the Bible from beginning to end was literally true, and divinely inspired. Other Christians, then and since, have looked on music, painting, ritual, sculpture, dogmatic theology, and priestly intercession as God-given means for the enrichment of their faith. But since for Puritans the Bible was the word of God, no other material aid seemed to them needful for the man who wished to attain a direct, individual, and personal relationship with his Creator.

The Old Testament forbade the worship of graven images, so it necessarily followed that no sincere Puritan could approve of religious art. But when the Presbyterians dominating Parliament sent out bands of zealots to destroy London's surviving heritage of medieval art, an element of political calculation was also responsible.

The pictures and statues then to be found in churches, and even on the streets, had come down from far-off days. They were works of art intended to teach Catholic doctrine to those unable to read. And London was still full of poor people unable to read a single word of the Bible. The Puritans believed that as soon as the crucifixes and the coloured images of Our Lady were smashed, the safe assumption was that religious instruction would come to the poor only from Calvinistic sermons and Presbyterian psalms.

On 25 April, an organized mob of fervent Puritans went into Westminster Abbey and St Margaret's (which by now it was the fashion to call merely Margaret's) to enact Parliament's will by smashing up all the gorgeous medieval stained glass.

On 2 May, the Puritans marched into the City, intending to wreck the Old Cross in Cheapside. The Cross was embellished with ancient religious sculptures, and on holidays the apprentices still observed the old custom of decking it with garlands. Once they saw what was happening, out from the shops in Cheapside swarmed a crowd of angry young men, each flourishing the club which in those days an apprentice kept under the counter to protect his master's property. They crowded around Cheapside Cross and got ready to fight for it. A troop of cavalry had to be sent charging down Cheapside to drive the apprentices off – and only

2 May 1643: the Puritans, helped by a troop of horses and two companies of foot, pull down the famous medieval Cross in Cheapside (John Freeman)

under armed protection were the Puritans able to smash the Cross to bits.

The horror of Catholicism at the back of ignorant people's minds – dating from the days of Bloody Mary – was to the Puritan leaders a useful way of keeping Londoners in check. Many of them had by now been taught to fear that one fine day the wild Irish Catholics would come across the sea and fight for King Charles. Puritan leaders like John Pym kept this fear alive with stories of the atrocities supposedly committed by the Irish, and, from time to time, by publicly hanging, and chopping into four pieces while still alive, some innocent Roman Catholic priest who had fallen into their hands.

Pym's agents used the anti-Catholic dodge in August 1643,

just as proposals for peace were to be debated in the House
of Commons. All over London Pym's men stuck up posters
warning that twenty thousand Papists were about to invade.

The poster told a clever lie, but gave unnerving public expression to a deep and dumb fear. For three generations now –
and the generations were to extend thereafter into centuries –
the Irish had been making brave and convulsive efforts to
throw off English rule by armed force.

Most of the Irish rebels were Roman Catholics, and they
gladly accepted aid from England's enemies. So the struggle
in Ireland – between English settlers, native Irish, and the
Presbyterian Scots sent not long ago by King James I to
colonize Ulster – was already taking on the merciless dimen-
sion, sadly familiar in our own day, of a religious war.

King Charles was King in Ireland too. Because his wife,
Henrietta Maria, was passionately Catholic, there were Irish
Catholics warm to his cause. And with England distracted by
civil conflict, the Irish rebels were winning hands down.

Charles would soon have to decide whether to tip the military balance decisively in his own favour by bringing over
native Irish troops – Roman Catholics – to fight on his side
in England. But since the arrival of tens of thousands of Irish
would obviously lose him the hearts of his English Protestant
supporters, King Charles might be tempted but was unlikely
to consent.

And Pym knew this very well. There was no real likelihood
whatever of twenty thousand Papists invading England, but
Pym, by playing on these secret fears, hoped to stampede
public opinion and paralyse the popular yearning for peace.
Yet even so, the vote for peace in an overwhelmingly Puritan
House of Commons was lost by only seven votes.

Women always bear the brunt of hardship in a war. Next
day a great crowd of decently dressed London housewives,

each with a white ribbon in her hat, surged into Palace Yard. They battered at the doors of Parliament for an hour, shouting 'Give us those traitors that were against peace! Give us that dog Pym!' They wanted to throw him in the Thames.

When the guards fired blank shots to frighten them off, the women riposted by throwing stones. The soldiers then loaded their muskets with ball and opened fire. They killed two men who were standing nearby, and the women's shouts rose to a scream.

Down from the City at a fast trot came a troop of Sir William Waller's cavalry, men of the army whose conduct against the Cavaliers at Roundway Down had been something less than heroic. The infuriated women went for these horsemen bare-handed. Some of the troopers lost their nerve and began hitting out with the edge of the sword. Several white-ribboned housewives were cut down, many trampled flat, and one was shot dead before they could all be driven back to their homes.

The Puritans in London, as they lost popular sympathy, began more and more to keep their ascendancy by armed force.

Had he pushed hard on London in the first week of August 1643, King Charles might have won the war. Waller's army was knocked out. Prince Rupert had taken Bristol. 'Black Tom' Fairfax had been driven from the West Riding. Puritan rule was beginning to irk ordinary Londoners. John Pym was sick. And though Pym had all this while been intriguing to win over the Presbyterian Scots, they had not yet agreed on a price for marching over the Border to stab Newcastle's army in the back. The King's time had clearly come.

The King's Cavalier officers would have been only too glad to ride full tilt across country and lord it again in plundered London. But the King himself was hesitant. As for the rank and file, the further they marched from their menaced homes in the north and west, the more they dragged their feet.

The King's newly enlisted regiments of Welshmen, for instance, were refusing to cross the Severn and join forces with Charles until Colonel Massey's Roundheads were driven out of Gloucester – from which they could easily raid South Wales.

Compared with the long wall and ring of forts around Bristol, Gloucester's defences were trivial, and twenty-three-year-old Puritan Colonel Edward Massey had only one regiment of trained soldiers. Prince Rupert wanted Gloucester taken quickly – by assault, not by a long-winded siege.

But assaulting a fortified city always cost lives. The King had been heart-stricken by the heavy Cavalier losses around the walls of Bristol. 'As gallant gentlemen as ever drew sword,' he grieved, 'lay upon the ground like rotten sheep.'

London at that moment was wide open to attack, and once London had fallen, the kingdom would again be the King's. Yet, because King Charles was tender-hearted, the decision was taken to put Gloucester through the safer but more time-wasting process of a formal siege.

Young Colonel Massey had for the past week been working alongside the citizens, spade in hand, to strengthen Gloucester's earthworks. Cathedral cities were usually Royalist, and the hearts of many Gloucester men might secretly incline to the King. But everyone in a threatened city had learned by now to dread the havoc that could be wreaked by plundering Cavaliers. By 10 August, Prince Rupert was ready to begin the siege. He called formally upon Colonel Massey to yield up Gloucester to the King – and Massey refused, knowing that he had the people behind him.

The news of young Edward Massey's bold defiance, coming after so much bad news, made hearts in London beat faster and caused a miraculous change of mood. Every shop in

Cheapside put up its shutters, as thousands of apprentices flocked to volunteer for special service. Five new regiments of foot and a thousand horse, nearly all London apprentices some of them not older than schoolboys, packed bread and cheese in their knapsacks and moved off westwards, weapons in hand, to join with the Earl of Essex.

On 24 August, Lord Essex reviewed his young volunteers on Hounslow Heath, 'riding with his hat off, and bowing to them'. His whole army by now numbered 15,000. Gloucester had already lived through twelve days of siege. Would it fall before the bold London lads marched over the hills to the rescue?

Prince Rupert had brought miners across from the Forest of Dean, and through two weeks of sunny weather – the only fine weeks that occurred in the wet summer of 1643 – they dug deep trenches, a quarter of a mile beyond the city wall, just out of range of the Gloucester musketeers. The miners then dug underground tunnels from their trenches to the walls, and under the walls Rupert stacked gunpowder.

On 24 August – the day Essex was reviewing his young volunteers on Hounslow Heath, hat in hand – Prince Rupert sent warning to Colonel Massey that unless he surrendered Gloucester, his fortifications would all be blown sky-high.

But a secret beacon up on the Cotswold Hills had signalled to the Roundheads the night before that help was on its way. Once more the young colonel refused to yield, though he knew his walls were mined. And luck was on his side. The weather later that night broke in a storm of rain. Rupert's trenches were flooded, and all his gunpowder was ruined.

On the clear evening of 5 September, Lord Essex reined in his charger on Prestbury Hill, lit his long clay pipe, and gazed into the distance at Gloucester's squat, impressive cathedral, crouched inside Colonel Massey's ring of makeshift earthworks, with the raw earth of the Royalist trenches farther out, and the gleaming River Severn beyond. His army of apprentices had fought their way past a strong force of cavalry sent by Rupert to cut them down. But had they come in time?

Essex fired a signal gun twice. From inside distant Gloucester came a puff of white smoke and then the reverberation of an answering gun. The city was holding out, and if the royal army was still down there, it would be taken between two hostile fires.

That night, under cover of darkness, the King's men marched off. King Charles had frittered away the best chance yet of regaining his kingdom. Next morning, at Painswick in the Cotswolds, the King paused to rest on a milestone. Though no longer a young man, he had been marching on foot, through the mud, to put heart in the royal infantry.

The little princes, Charles and James, came shyly up to their father to ask him when they were going home. Sadly, the King told them 'I have no home to go to.' The King had sensed that the tide of war had turned.

Prince Rupert told King Charles that despite the long delay at Gloucester there was still one good chance left. If the royal army could march across England fast enough to get between Essex's army and its base in London, Essex and his 15,000 men could be brought to battle. If the King's men could knock out Essex and the best of the trained bands as they had already dealt with Waller, Parliament would be left with no army. The Peace Party in the House of Commons would triumph, and London would open her gates to the King.

Essex was well aware of the danger, too. But he was not by nature an energetic man, and his young apprentices were hungry. When the bread and cheese in their knapsacks were gone they lived off blackberries and nuts from the hedgerows. At last they managed to round up a flock of Cotswold sheep, which they drove before them on the march and turned into hot mutton at suppertime. Parliament's army was marching back home to London at the pace of those sheep.

The two armies, slowly approaching, were only ten miles apart by 17 September. By now they were racing each other for Newbury, a Puritan cloth town perched at the end of the chalk downs, which commanded the road along the Thames valley into London.

On the evening of 19 September 1643, Parliamentary quartermasters riding ahead of their army were the first to reach Newbury. Food and supplies had been hospitably stocked there, in readiness for the Roundheads' arrival. But Essex's men at this moment were a dragging column ten miles long, and several hours' march to the westward.

The Roundhead quartermasters were riding busily up and down the streets of Newbury, chalking doors to mark billets for their troops, when down the main road came the thundering hooves of Prince Rupert's Cavaliers.

A few of the quartermasters were captured, others got away on horseback under a hail of pistol bullets and managed to reach their army in time to give warning. The Earl of Essex was marching into a trap. The King had got to Newbury first. The only way home was to fight.

The battle of Newbury was fought over rolling grassy hillsides intersected by deep lanes. The armies were fairly matched, the King being as usual the stronger in cavalry. But Lord Essex's infantry, commanded by that tough and wise old soldier Philip Skippon, was probably the best in all England – stout-hearted 'prentice lads who had learned their drill thoroughly in the London trained bands.

The footsoldiers in the King's army, led by Sir Jacob Astley, were simple countrymen, fretful at being such a long way from home, and sometimes resentful at not being paid. The Royalists were also short of gunpowder. Much had been wasted at Gloucester.

Lord Essex decided to give battle at five next morning. During the night he sent Philip Skippon with two field-pieces and a force of good infantry to occupy a dome-shaped hill nearby. Round Hill dominated the high ground near Wash Common, where the main clash between the two armies was bound to take place. Its slopes were crisscrossed with the hedges of small fields and market gardens, where footsoldiers could hope to make a stand against even the best cavalry.

As the sun came up, old Philip Skippon, with his long experience of battles in the Dutch wars, smiled grimly at the sight of Rupert's horse streaming across Wash Common. The King's generals, too, had grasped the fact that the battle would be won by the side that held Round Hill – but they had reached this conclusion several hours too late.

The King's infantry was sent to fight its way obstinately up the slopes of Round Hill, the Cavaliers helping footsoldiers upward by repeated flank charges on Skippon's pikemen and musketeers. The Royalists were obliged to push up the hill hedge by hedge. Each small field was bristling with Roundhead pikes, and behind each hedge were the files, six deep, of trained bands of musketeers.

On the parade ground of the City of London, in their long summer evenings after work, Philip Skippon had drilled his young men impeccably in rolling fire. The young musketeer at the front of a file took careful aim at his enemy. He fired his shot, and hastened to the rear of his file to reload. As with busy fingers he charged his weapon with powder and ball, five more shots were fired by the men in front of him. And there he was, in the front rank again, and with a loaded weapon in his hand, ready to aim at another living target.

The murderous, expert chatter of this Roundhead fusillade from walls and hedgerows went on all day long. Royalist musketeers got off only one shot to the Roundheads' three, and their powder was running low.

There were twenty guns in the royal artillery park. They helped the obstinate Cavalier attack by blasting gaps in the living defence of Round Hill, one cavalryman observing 'a whole file of men, six deep, with all their heads struck off by one cannon shot of ours'. But Skippon's two light field guns on the crest of the hill did damage too – and the King's big guns swallowed up powder.

This gruelling, grinding battle outside Newbury raged without pause from dawn until ten at night. One stupendous Cavalier charge, bearing all before it, thundered all the way up Round Hill to the very mouths of Skippon's guns, only to be pushed downhill again, like the largest wave coming up the beach at high tide and falling back. Against the implacable resistance of the London lads, the Cavalier tide ebbed. By darkness, when the gunfire had faded, Skippon's trained bands still held Round Hill.

Late that night, as carts full of dead and dying rumbled into Newbury, King Charles held a council of war. Lord Percy, as General of the Artillery, reported that eighty barrels of powder had been spent during the long day's fight. There were only ten full powder barrels left. To attack Round Hill next day, against the rolling fire of those musketeers with nothing but cold steel, would condemn the royal army to destruction. The King called off the battle.

As Lord Essex marched his men rapidly off down the road to London, Prince Rupert's horsemen went after them. At Aldermaston he managed to mount a skilful ambush, but the pikemen of the rearguard fought him off. Amid loud enthusiasm, the Roundhead army entered London. The victorious youngsters marched with pike and musket through the city, laurels in their hats. Next day most of them were back behind their shop counters, politely serving customers.

The King had lost his best chance, but it was no fault of the Cavaliers. Gentlemen on horseback who fought in the royal cause were courageous, if sometimes ill disciplined. Those King's men who fought from conviction would go on to the bitter end. But the rank and file – the poor foot, and those cavalry troopers and dragoons who had enlisted only for their pay – were no longer willing to match their officers in blind courage. As Sir John Byron wrote scathingly after the battle of Newbury, 'Had not our foot played the poltroons extremely that day, we in all probability had set a period to the war.'

CHAPTER SIX

Insolent Rebels

> If we beat the King ninety times, yet he is King still ... but
> if the King beat us once, we shall be all hanged, and our
> posterity made slaves – THE EARL OF MANCHESTER
> (formerly Lord Mandeville) as Major-General of the
> Eastern Association

ON 8 December 1643, when they heard of John Pym's death, the Royalists at Oxford lit bonfires in the streets. But Parliament buried Pym in Henry VII's chapel in Westminster Abbey, amid the Kings and Queens of England. Since John Pym had spent his entire estate in the Puritan cause and had died in debt, Parliament voted his heirs £10,000 a year in land – nowadays worth more than ten times as much, and a princely fortune.

Sir Henry Vane, a young man of thirty who up to now had been the Earl of Warwick's right-hand man as organizer of the navy, took John Pym's place as leader of the party in Parliament determined to fight the war to a finish.

Harry Vane, one of the few Puritan leaders not to enrich himself by some means or other during the war, was a fair-haired young man with a big nose, prominent pale eyes, and irregular features. He could be wittily charming when charm served his purpose. But in difficult negotiations, Vane was as stone-faced as a poker player, quick to discover his opponents' intentions, slow to disclose his own.

Young Harry Vane had been at the same school, Westminster, as Sir Arthur Haselrig. The headmaster there, a sarcastic wit called Lambert Osbaldestone, had discussed his

Puritan opinions openly with the boys, even in the years when King Charles ruled without a Parliament, and such frankness could be dangerous. For the crime of calling Archbishop Laud 'a little meddling hocus-pocus', Lambert Osbaldestone had been fined £10,000, and sentenced to be nailed by his ears to the pillory in front of all his pupils. But Osbaldestone escaped from the Archbishop's men in the nick of time. In London there were plenty of Puritan houses where he could safely hide.

Because his father was a high official at the King's court, a splendid career lay open to Harry Vane. But the arguments at Westminster School had made him think seriously about religion. While he was a student he underwent a religious conversion similar to that of Oliver Cromwell, who became his close friend. These two men rejected not only the King's Anglicanism and the Queen's Catholicism, but also the Presbyterianism of the King's more prominent enemies. Vane became an Independent and a mystic. He was so passionately concerned with religious freedom, in fact, that when he was only twenty-two he turned his back on the temptations at the court of King Charles and, taking John Pym's advice, crossed the Atlantic in *Abigail* with 220 other Puritan emigrants and a cargo of cattle, to seek a new life in Massachusetts.

Harry Vane made close friends in New England with a minister called Roger Williams, who shared his unorthodox religious beliefs. When Roger Williams was banished from Massachusetts for asserting, among other heresies, that the King of England had no right to make grants of land rightfully belonging to the Indians, he travelled south into the wilderness and went to live with Miantonimo, sachem of the Narragansetts.

On 24 March 1636, when he was only twenty-three, Harry Vane was elected Governor of Massachusetts. Soon after, the

war with the Pequot Indians threatened. Many New Englanders were for crushing the Indians at once with brute
force. But Harry Vane, though willing enough to fight if he
had no choice, wanted to see first if the Indians could be won
over by diplomacy. He knew that by now Roger Williams
was fluent in the Indian tongues, and that the Pequots were
trying to combine forces with the Narragansetts.

Roger Williams volunteered to cross the open sea alone in
a canoe, and go to the Narragansett village and plead with
them. By patient explanation he won the Narragansetts away
from the idea of attacking the New England settlements. 'God
wonderfully preserved me,' he wrote, 'and helped me break
in pieces the Pequots' negotiation and design.'

By October, young Harry Vane and Roger Williams had
managed to make a treaty with their disunited enemies that
saved Massachusetts from a large-scale Indian war. But both
of these men were irked by the limitations on religious freedom imposed by church leaders in Massachusetts. After his
year of office young Vane went back to England and was
elected to Parliament as a supporter of John Pym.

The young New England governor, who had learned his
job as a political leader on the frontier of civilization, was
now spokesman for the radical side in England's civil war.
His American experiences were to stand him in good stead.
In old England, just as in New England, strange ideas of civil
and religious liberty were entering men's minds.

The Roundhead cause had suffered so many setbacks lately
that subtle diplomacy would be needed to bring the Scots to
terms and get them to send an army to Parliament's aid. For
£30,000 per month, the Scots were willing to send an army
into England, but they wanted something else besides money.
They were asking that all the English loyal to Parliament
should swear to the Covenant, an oath accepting the strict

principles of Calvinism. England must then agree to reorganize her church on a Presbyterian model, without bishops.

Obliging a man to swear a forced oath is not the best way to change his deepest beliefs, but the Scots were desperately anxious. Scotland was then a very poor country with a small population. In the Scottish Lowlands, peasant and merchant, laird and nobleman alike were Presbyterian. The Kirk (the Church of Scotland) was the centre of their national existence.

Only a few years earlier the Scots had defied King Charles when, through his bishops, he had tried to impose on them the Anglican prayer-book and liturgy, and they had defeated an English army sent against them by the King to break their will by force. To Scotland, therefore, the Covenant was a symbol of national determination. The only English government the Scots were prepared henceforth to trust was one accepting the same religious basis as their own.

To the Presbyterian Scots, the Independents – like Cromwell and Lilburne – now raising their heads in England were abhorrent as King Charles and his Anglican prayer-book had been a few years before. Only if all the English Roundheads swore to the Covenant would a Scottish army cross the border and in Pym's last days Harry Vane was sent north to manage matters.

In its Scottish form, the Covenant was more than most Roundheads could swallow, but Harry Vane found a way. The Scots have a reputation for being severely logical, whereas the English are often inconsistent and even muddle-headed. Into the English version of the Covenant, Harry Vane managed to slip a clause that sounded innocent, but could be read any number of ways. Most English dissenters, even though they might have inner scruples, could now sign the oath without too much offence to their consciences. Now the Scots would send an army, but only at the price of forcing upon many of those who had taken up arms in the Parliamentary cause an act of deliberate hypocrisy.

From now on 'Presbyterian' was to be more than ever a party label, and those who wanted a Presbyterian organization of England's church would speak more from political expediency than religious conviction. The high principles with which both sides had first gone to war had begun to get shopworn.

Over the water in Ireland, the Roman Catholic Irish rebels, having reconquered nine-tenths of their own country, had at last obliged the English army fighting them to call a truce.

If the English soldiers in Ireland could be brought back to England to fight in King Charles's cause, that would cancel out the advantage Parliament was hoping to gain from its army of Presbyterian Scots.

There could hardly be an objection to King Charles's employing English soldiers who up to now had been fighting the Irish. But his Puritan enemies let it be known that Irish Roman Catholics themselves would be taking a hand in the English Civil War. To many English Protestants, the mere off-chance of this happening was a nightmare.

At the beginning of the Irish rising, four thousand Protestant settlers in Ireland had been put to the sword – an ugly fact that Pym's followers had drummed into men's minds ever since. But behind this artificially whipped-up fear that tens of thousands of Irish Catholics with long knives and shaggy hair might come over one dark night and slaughter all good English Protestants in their beds lay a secret greed for Irish land.

In 1641, when King Charles had been obliged to raise an army to put down the rebellion of his Irish subjects, the City of London had offered to find money for him privately, without the need for new and unpopular taxes. But a bargain was struck that once the Roman Catholic Irish had been defeated, estates in Ireland amounting to 2·5 million acres would be confiscated by the victors and divided among London shareholders.

Puritan leaders had taken a large financial interest in this murky enterprise, and important men among the Presbyterian Scots were also deep in the speculation. Any Irishman falling into Parliamentary hands would therefore find himself facing men easily able to give a religious gloss to their fear and greed. He could hardly expect fair play.

Early in 1644, for example, Captain Richard Swanley, patrolling the Pembrokeshire coast, captured a vessel with 150 soldiers aboard under the Royalist Colonel Willoughby. They were presumed to be coming back from Ireland to serve King Charles.

The English among the prisoners were given a chance to save their lives – they could swear the Covenant and take service under Parliament. But the seventy Irish soldiers were tied back to back and thrown alive into the sea 'to wash from them the blood of the Protestants that was upon them'. And on 4 June 1644, the gallant Captain Swanley was summoned to the bar of the House of Commons, where many of the members who applauded him had a financial interest in forfeited Irish estates, to receive a gold medal for his 'services in Pembrokeshire'.

East Anglia, too, had a rebel tradition. Ninety years before, Jack Ket had led the men of Norfolk in England's last big peasant revolt. Every kind of religious dissent and independent belief flourished in East Anglia.

Different versions of Protestantism had arrived with the French Huguenots and with the thousands of Dutchmen who had fled from Spanish persecution in the Low Countries.

The Bible-reading East Anglian yeoman often combined farming with weaving special kinds of woollen cloth. But in recent years the continental wars had spoiled his market for cloth, so that many had gone to seek a better chance in New England. The map of present-day New England is littered with the names of towns and villages from England's eastern counties.

East Anglians had watched with fervent interest the long rearguard action that Protestants on the continent of Europe had been fighting against Catholic kings and princes. They had seen their cause go down to defeat almost everywhere except among the Dutch. And all East Anglians had some relative in America, where a new world was slowly being hacked out of the wilderness. Small wonder they were all heart and soul in Parliament's war.

Oliver Cromwell, who had worked a farm in the Fen country, could talk to his East Anglian cavalry on their own terms, and he was well aware that he must tolerate and respect their religious differences. But in return for this freedom of belief they gave him strict obedience as soldiers. Cavaliers in the heat of battle often disregarded their orders, through pride or love of plunder, but the troopers in Cromwell's regiment were exemplary in their discipline because each man's obedience was voluntary and based on his own self-control. On the Puritan side, soldiers of a new type were emerging.

Many of Cromwell's recruits believed not merely that the Bible was literally true, but that biblical prophecies of a Chosen People and a Promised Land and a Second Coming applied most of all to England. An expectation grew among them that victory in the cause would bring a new heaven and a new earth – a world of neither rich nor poor, ruled by the godly, where each man would have his own farm or his own trade. They had been learning their business as troopers in skirmishes against Cavaliers pressing down on East Anglia from the north. But they were as yet untested in battle.

On 19 January 1644, a Scots army of 18,000 foot and 3,000 horse commanded by a wrinkled, bandy-legged old soldier called Lord Leven, who had been a famous general in the German wars, crossed into England. The frost was so intense that they crossed the River Tweed on ice, and it bore the weight of horse and gun.

Each regiment of Leven's army was organized like a Kirk session in a Scottish parish, with its own Presbyterian minister and lay elders. Prayers were said in the army twice a day, and on the Sabbath there were sermons morning and evening. Soldiers who used bad language lost their pay and were obliged to make 'public repentance in the midst of the congregation'. Plundering and being drunk on guard were offences punishable by death.

This invasion of England by a Scottish army gave Cromwell his chance to overawe Cambridge University, of which he had once been a member. Twelve heads of House and 181 Fellows or university officials, men who would rather lose their livelihood than swear to a Covenant in which they did not believe, were driven out of the university. Their jobs were given to Puritans.

A review of troops was held in King's College Chapel by Lieutenant-General Lawrence Crawford, a rather vain professional soldier who had fought well against the papists in Ireland. The Anglican prayer-book was publicly torn to pieces in St Mary's. Cambridge colleges were turned into barracks or prisons.

Zealous Puritans went round making sure that all the stained glass in the college chapels had been smashed.

Roundhead soldiers breaking altar rails, pulling down a religious painting and taking away a crucifix (John Freeman)

Cromwell himself gave the order to chop up the famous wood-carvings in St Mary's. Stained glass and graven images were superstitious. For the Puritans, the Bible was enough.

Across the Atlantic, the little English-speaking colonies down the eastern coastline reflected as in a mirror the deadly struggle at home in England.

Sir William Berkeley was notorious for having once said of Virginia, the colony he governed for the King, 'I thank God there are no free schools, or printing, and I hope we shall not have, these hundred years.' Virginia was then a colony of big tobacco plantations of up to five thousand acres, on which black slaves were beginning to take the place of poor Englishmen who had come out to Virginia as indentured labourers.

Though Sir William Berkeley did his best to help the King

with money, and though the Virginian planters were Royalists at heart, they were never very active in the King's cause. In 1644 there was a fight in the Chesapeake between a Parliament ship from London and a King's ship from Bristol. The Indians watched it and decided the time had come to rise up, 'because they saw the English took all their land from them'. When three hundred Virginians had been massacred, the English Parliament shipped over a cargo of arms 'for the supply and defence and relief of the planters of Virginia' – even though the Virginians were Cavaliers.

Though Maryland was in the hands of the Roman Catholic Lord Baltimore, it was so much the most tolerant of England's North American colonies that when, in 1643, nonconformist Protestants were expelled from Virginia, they found a welcome across the Potomac River in Maryland.

But the peaceful life in Maryland ended in 1644, when the colony was invaded by armed men claiming to be Protestant supporters of the Parliamentary cause. They were led by Richard Ingle, the Puritan captain of the merchantman *Reformation*, and William Claiborne, who had another quarrel with Lord Baltimore.

Though Captain Ingle later tried to persuade Parliament that when his men robbed 'papists and malignants' in Maryland it was simply to relieve the wants of poor Protestants, what most keenly interested Ingle and Claiborne in the two years they ruled the roost in Maryland was plunder. They used religion as a cloak for greed.

Many Marylanders in these bad times had fled to their friends in Virginia. From among them Governor Calvert raised a small armed force, and in the winter of 1646–7 he marched back home to throw out Ingle and Claiborne. But Maryland's troubles were not over. Ingle had ways to make his voice heard in London, and in 1650 he tried to persuade Parliament to send out a fleet and crush the papists and

Royalists dwelling on the banks of the Potomac. At last, in 1653, a government submissive to Cromwell was elected in Maryland – a colony that had never openly supported King Charles – by the simple expedient of denying to the great number of Roman Catholics there the right to vote or stand for office.

For puritanical Massachusetts, the dominant colony in New England, the Civil War broke out in the nick of time, because King Charles had been threatening to take away the colony's charter. As Governor Winthrop put it, 'the disorders of the mother country were the safeguard of the infant liberties of New England'.

New England was a land of small farmers, with no class of large landowners who from tradition supported the King, and the first few months of the Civil War had been difficult. Puritans in England were no longer selling all they owned and crossing the Atlantic; they were no longer pouring by tens of thousands into New England, bringing all their money with them. Indeed, the drift was the other way. Many Puritans in the colonies sold what they owned and went back home to fight in the Parliamentary cause.

'Our supplies from England failing,' wrote Winthrop, 'men began to look about them.' Yankee ingenuity was put to the test. The men in Massachusetts 'fell to the manufacture of cotton, whereof we had store from Barbados'.

Young America was learning to industrialize. New water mills were grinding corn and sawing timber. In April 1643, the first ship built in Boston, the 160-ton *Trial*, sailed across to Spain with salt fish and brought back a useful cargo of iron, oil, wine, and fruit. New Englanders were proving that most of the things England had once provided for her colonies could be made or traded for. New England, though not yet independent, was at least much less dependent than it had been before the Civil War.

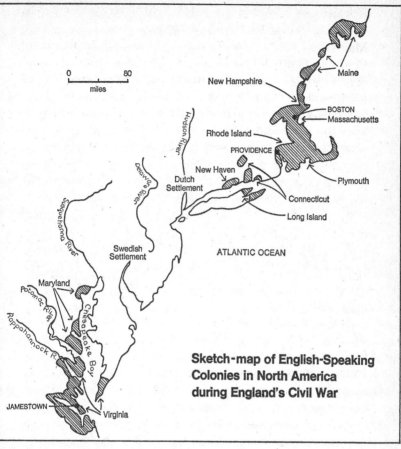

Sketch-map of English-Speaking Colonies in North America during England's Civil War

The Puritan supporters of Parliament in New England were separated from the Cavaliers in Virginia not only by hundreds of miles of coastline but by Dutch settlements on the Hudson River and Swedish settlements on the Delaware River

Sir Henry Vane's friend, Roger Williams, had already been driven out from Massachusetts to Rhode Island for advocating that 'the civil magistrate should restrain crime, but never control opinion'. In Rhode Island he was the leading spirit in a new colony where civil liberty and religious freedom could more readily be enjoyed.

Indeed, New Englanders were soon to discover that there was more religious and political liberty back in insurrectionary England than in Massachusetts, where only members of the Calvinistic Church were allowed to vote. In 1646, 'some who lately came from England, where such vast liberty is allowed', presented a petition to the authorities in Massachusetts, demanding the vote for the thousands of citizens in the colony who were not church members. Not only was the petition rejected, but when the petitioners tried to appeal to the English Parliament, they were fined and imprisoned.

In 1644 Baptists were banished by law from Massachusetts, though in England many Baptists were high-ranking officers in the Parliament's army. In 1648, a Baptist called Obadiah Holmes, who defied this law, was flogged thirty strokes with a cat of three tails. Independence could work both ways.

And what if little Rhode Island – the best place in New England for a Baptist or a Jew or a discontented servant to flee for refuge – were swallowed up by its less tolerant neighbours? Unkind tongues in Boston were already nicknaming Roger Williams's colony 'Rogue Island', and complaining that he gave sanctuary there to men wanted by the law.

Parliament in London might in this case help to put freedom in America on a firmer foundation. In Providence, Portsmouth, and Newport, the pioneers decided to send Roger Williams to London to enlist the help of his old friend Harry Vane. They sought a charter that would give legal recognition to the Providence Plantation and thereby protect their right to freedom of belief.

Roger Williams reached London during the bitter winter of 1643–4. No chimneys in the great city were smoking, and the poorer Londoners shuddered with cold and hunger. The port of Newcastle, which in winter used to send seacoal to London, was still firmly in the grip of the King's northern army.

Roger Williams had an intricate diplomatic mission to accomplish, but he managed to combine it with his religious duty to ease distress among the London poor. Soon, prodded by Roger Williams, Parliament agreed to get fires for poor families by cutting down all the trees within thirty miles of London. They began with the handsome forest trees in Windsor Great Park – which belonged to King Charles. And on 14 March 1644, a Parliamentary committee headed by the piratical Earl of Warwick granted Rhode Island a charter guaranteeing her territorial integrity and liberty of conscience.

The King had advanced Lord Newcastle from Earl to the rank of Marquess after his victory over Fairfax at Adwalton Moor. But long-haired poetic Lord Newcastle, though a splendid fellow in so many other ways, was not much of a leader for an army of discontented levies. The royal army in the north was melting away. In the autumn of 1643, in one month alone, half his men went home.

As Lord Leven came over the Border with a Scottish army 21,000 strong, Lord Newcastle's force was reduced to 3,000 rather badly armed cavalry and 5,000 foot, including his famous Whitecoats. The new Marquess of Newcastle now had two enemies to contend with. Lord Leven's Scots were coming down from the north, and the Roundheads were coming up from the south.

Newcastle managed to convince himself that his army might be good enough to deal with either of these two enemies separately, but not both at once. If he had only the English Roundheads to deal with, the advance on London from the north could well begin, the other jaw of the nut-cracker start at last to close, and the King's grand strategy for regaining his capital city and, with it, his throne become a reality. On 16 February 1644, Lord Newcastle wrote opti-mistically to King Charles 'If your Majesty beat the Scots, your game is absolutely won.'

King Charles decided to send off his young nephew Rupert to save the royal cause in the north. King Charles never had money to spare to reward his faithful generals, but titles of honour cost him nothing, and pleased others very much. So he dubbed Rupert with a new title, Duke of Cumberland ('of Plunderland' sneered the Roundheads).

The Royalist fortress of Newark Castle, commanding the highway north and south, was menaced by 7,000 Parlia-mentary troops, led by Sir John Meldrum. Prince Rupert and his Cavaliers moved on Newark, and so rapidly that Sir John at first refused to believe that the Cavaliers could be within striking distance. Rupert smuggled a cryptic letter into Newark Castle, addressed to the Governor, Sir Richard Byron. His message read 'Let the old Drum be beaten early on the morrow morning', and Sir Richard had the wit to understand what the Prince was hinting.

Next day Sir Richard Byron made a bold sortie from Newark Castle on Sir John Meldrum and his 7,000 Round-heads, which coincided with a whirlwind attack by Prince Rupert's Cavaliers.

Meldrum surrendered on terms, and Prince Rupert's little army marched north, the better equipped by 4,000 captured muskets, 4,000 pistols, 50 barrels of gunpowder, and 15 guns. His next task was to break the power of the Puritans in Lancashire. Then he could join forces with Lord Newcastle, and the great sweep south might begin.

*

Until now, the royal cause in Lancashire had been represented by Lord Derby, the biggest landowner in the country,
a man detested by his tenantry as cruel and mistrusted for
his cowardice. In the spring of 1643, after a smaller Roundhead force had beaten Lord Derby at Whalley Abbey, the
country folk turned on him with scythes and flails, and Lord
Derby had fled to the safety of his private island, the Isle of
Man. His wife Charlotte was left behind in Lancashire to
defend Lord Derby's great country mansion of Lathom
House.

The Countess of Derby, a French aristocrat with Crusader
blood in her veins, had been born Charlotte de la Tremouille.
She was no beauty, but she brought her unpleasant English
husband an enormous dowry – equivalent in present-day
terms to more than a quarter of a million pounds sterling.

This large-limbed, intrepid Frenchwoman with glittering
eyes and biting tongue had left her own sunny countryside to
live with a dismal and sometimes cruel husband in Lathom
House, a huge, damp stone mansion, inside a moat twenty-
four feet wide. Lathom House was built on a marsh amid
insignificant hills, in a countryside where it never stopped
raining.

Sir Thomas Fairfax began campaigning across Lancashire
and Cheshire, driving the King's men before him. Lathom
House, within its marsh, with its nine stone towers, became
the one safe Cavalier refuge. From there the defeated Royalists raided and plundered the countryside around. Com-
plaints from the pillaged countryfolk poured in, and on 24
February 1644, in Puritan Manchester, the Lancashire
County Committee decided on a siege.

Word of their threat reached Lady Derby next day. She
had brought in all the food and munitions her men could
lay their hands on, and by the time Sir Thomas Fairfax and

his Roundhead soldiers had marched up from Bolton and Wigan on 27 February she was ready for them.

Lathom House was a stronghold. In each of its nine towers were half a dozen small cannon, covering each approach from the surrounding hills across the marsh. Sixteen musketeers, all crack shots, also kept watch in the towers. The 300 men in the garrison were organized into half-companies, which did twelve-hour stints of guard duty. They could never be taken by surprise.

On Sunday, 10 March, a party of Lord Derby's tenantry arrived at the Roundhead camp and humbly asked Sir Thomas Fairfax if they might be allowed to go into Lathom House and plead with the Countess to be sensible. The Countess had already given Black Tom a piece of her mind, informing him that 'though a woman and a stranger, divorced of her friends and robbed of her estate, she was ready to receive their utmost violence, trusting in God for both Protection and Deliverance.' Black Tom, who was anxious not to tie down thousands of his men in a long siege, let the Countess's folk go through the fortified gateway of the big house. Once inside, they gleefully joined forces with the garrison.

Fairfax was ready to let the people in Lathom House leave with all their goods and weapons if they would simply promise never to use them later against Parliament. These were generous terms, but the Countess rejected them with contempt. Her three hundred followers were soon giving a very busy time to three thousand Roundhead soldiers.

Fairfax marched away to besiege York, and gave command in the siege to Colonel Alexander Rigby, Puritan Member of Parliament for Wigan. But for Rigby to send any of his men within gunshot of the marksmen in those nine towers was suicidal..

Colonel Rigby had no siege guns heavy enough to make

a breach in the six-foot-thick stone walls of Lathom House. His largest piece was a mortar loading eight-pound shot. With this he managed to knock out the clock in the clocktower, and to plump a couple of cannonballs through Lady Derby's bedroom.

At this affront, the Countess's blood was up. Twelve horses were eating their heads off in the stables of Lathom House. They were harnessed to a sled, and at four in the morning of 26 April, a force of picked men under Captain Chisenhale sallied out with sled and horsemen from the eastern gate. They drove the Roundhead artillerymen from their entrenchments at sword point. They tipped the heavy mortar on to the sled and managed to drag it back across the drawbridge and into their own courtyard.

The spirited handful of Cavalier defenders gave the Roundheads no breathing space. Colonel Rigby reported glumly to his committee 'We are obliged to repel them five or six times a night.' And by now, the thrifty Puritans of the Manchester committee were reaching deep into their pockets. The siege of Lathom House was costing them £4,627 6s. 4d. a week, with each town in Parliamentary Lancashire being levied to pay its share.

News reached the Countess at the end of May that her husband had left the safety of his private island at last to join Prince Rupert. The Prince with 8,000 men, mostly cavalry, was marching up fast to relieve Lathom House. The Lancashire Roundheads had already lost 500 men. During the past five or six days, fighting around the stronghold had petered out. After weeks of risking their lives night and day in the incessant rain, Rigby's men had been deserting to their homes.

When Colonel Rigby heard that Prince Rupert was coming down on him, he marched away the remnant of his men to Bolton, the nearest Puritan town, but the day after he and

his men reached it, Prince Rupert and his army appeared outside. Bolton was exactly what the Cavaliers liked best – a
psalm-singing puritanical cloth town, full of enemies and
full of plunder.

The first Cavalier attack – in drenching rain – was beaten
back valiantly by Bolton's garrison at a cost to Rupert of 200
men. In anger the Prince gave orders to storm the town and
refuse all quarter. Lord Derby led the attack from one side,
and Rupert himself from the other.

The Roundheads were overwhelmed, and this time the
Cavaliers showed no mercy. They put to the sword 1,600 of
their Puritan enemies, and after that the couple of hundred
Roundheads who managed to survive this massacre were
tied together humiliatingly, two by two, and led off as
prisoners. Bolton was then very thoroughly plundered.

Colonel Rigby, who happened to have overheard the
Royalist password, managed to pass himself off as a Cavalier
and to escape on horseback across the moors, to join Fairfax
in Yorkshire. Lord Derby himself was judged to have done
the worst deed of the day. He obliged a former servant of
his, a Parliamentary captain called Booth, to kneel before
him and plead for mercy, and as soon as the words were in
the man's mouth, he ran his sword through him in cold
blood.

For this and other misdeeds, Lord Derby's name was
written high on Parliament's list of men to be denied all
pardon. Seven years later, when the fighting was over, Lord
Derby was put to death in the Bolton market place, with
the men and women his soldiers had ravished and plundered
looking on.

In a single week, Prince Rupert's whirlwind campaign had
overrun Lancashire for the King. And what was the Prince
to do next? Rupert had a letter of confidential instructions,

written out for him by King Charles, and to his dying day he carried this letter always in his pocket, to justify himself.

Should he go on defeating his Roundhead enemy here and there piecemeal, or seek to fight a decisive battle? The next urgent task was to relieve the cathedral city of York, the royal headquarters in the north, under siege by an allied force of Scots and Roundheads. But the King's letter contained the following fatal words: 'If York be relieved and you beat the rebel's army of Both Kingdoms, which are before it ...'

Sir John Culpeper, a royal adviser who knew Prince Rupert's headstrong nature well, was shown a copy of this letter. He exclaimed to King Charles 'Before God you are undone, for upon this peremptory order he will fight whatever comes on't.'

CHAPTER SEVEN

Stubble to our Swords

We never charged but we routed the enemy ... God made them as stubble to our swords – OLIVER CROMWELL, after commanding the Eastern Association horse at Marston Moor

CAMPED around the walled cathedral city of York, there were by now three allied armies loyal to Parliament. Sir Thomas Fairfax's northcountrymen were there, and Lord Leven's Scots, and the men of the Eastern Association, the best of them raised and trained by Oliver Cromwell. Parliament mistrusted the radicals of East Anglia, so command of this third army had been given to a Puritan peer called Lord Manchester, a man of no great military talent who earlier, as Lord Mandeville, had taken his chances with the Five Members.

Inside York these allies were cooping up the army of that extravagant grandee, the Marquess of Newcastle. The Royalists were trapped inside York, but the Parliamentarians around the city were pinned down by the siege too, much as, earlier, King Charles and Prince Rupert had been pinned down at the siege of Gloucester.

Lord Eythin, an unpleasant mercenary with long military experience in Germany, whom Lord Newcastle kept as his tame general, had been organizing resistance inside the walls of York with great efficiency. All the foodstuffs in the Royalist city were placed in one store, each man's daily ration being 'a mutchkin of beans, an ounce of butter, and a penny loaf.'

The Parliamentarians' first attempt to force a breach in York's ancient walls was a failure. The Roundheads began by mining St Mary's Tower – much as Rupert had mined the walls of Gloucester. But at York their failure was due, not to wet weather, but to the vanity of Lieutenant-General Lawrence Crawford. So as to be the first inside the city, Crawford sprang the mine without warning the other Parliamentary generals, and in the breach his attacking troops were overpowered.

Sir Thomas Fairfax had lived before the war at Nunappleton House, just outside York. He had long been paying a scholar called Roger Dodsworth to copy out the ancient manuscripts which were preserved in St Mary's Tower, and which Crawford's gunpowder had blown sky-high. Black Tom now offered a reward to any soldier who could find a parchment among the rubble. Risking their necks within gunshot of the enemy, his men rescued a few of the valuable documents, including a famous charter granted by Athelstan.

After his lightning victories in Lancashire, Prince Rupert was expected soon to burst over the Pennines into Yorkshire. Harry Vane, the young ex-governor of Massachusetts, was sent up to York to find out how the generals intended to meet this threat from Prince Rupert. He also had a secret proposal to make, which might end the war quickly, yet give Parliament much of what it had been fighting for.

King Charles was known by now to be a noble-spirited but self-willed man with one fixed idea: that he had been endowed with his regal powers by God. No pressure or bargaining was likely to make him yield this God-given authority to Parliament.

But suppose King Charles could be deposed, and some other, more pliable, King of the blood royal crowned in his place? The young Prince of Wales was now fourteen. Might he not make a puppet king? If not, Harry Vane had yet another candidate up his sleeve.

Charles Louis, the Elector Palatine, who was Prince Rupert's elder brother, was a rather limp character, but at least he was a devout Calvinist. Charles Louis's mother and father had lost their kingdom of Bohemia – might he not be happy to accept the throne of England?

Harry Vane's scheme was clever and well-intentioned. He wanted to avoid bloodshed. But though he put forward the secret plan with all his great diplomatic skill, his proposals shocked the army leaders. The Scottish generals answered bluntly that they had no authority to discuss such a notion. King Charles was a Scot, and his fellow-countrymen had by no means given up all hope of bending him to their will. Oliver Cromwell liked the idea, but the other English generals were horrified – most of all the Earl of Manchester.

For the peers among the Roundhead war leaders – men like Manchester, Essex, or Warwick – as well as for rich Presbyterians like Holles or Waller, to cast King Charles aside was not only a shocking idea, but might prove dangerous. Such men as they were of importance in the world thanks only to a complicated structure of titles, privileges, and landed property. Their right to their own estates and titles was no better than the King's right to his throne. Arms had already been put into the hands of the land-hungry common people of England. And if England's rightful King was unceremoniously thrust aside, whose turn might come next?

An aristocratic cavalry officer called Lord George Goring, who had often hunted the fox over the Yorkshire moors, led Rupert's cavalry by a clever roundabout route towards York, swinging them north at Knaresborough and crossing the River Swale at Thornton Bridge, a long way upstream. The sudden appearance outside York of Prince Rupert and his

Cavaliers, arriving from such an unexpected direction, shocked the Parliamentarians out of their wits.

The generals commanding the three allied armies pulled their 25,000 men out so fast that they left their heavy siege guns behind, not to mention 4,000 pairs of boots. Newcastle's poverty-stricken infantrymen burst out of York and ran joyously towards this pile of boots. Many of them had been serving barefoot.

When Lord Newcastle and Prince Rupert joined forces, the Prince commanded 17,000 men. Royalists and Roundheads had each about the same number of cavalry, but there was more Roundhead infantry. If it came to a battle, the King's men would be fighting against odds, horse and foot combined, of roughly three to two.

Would Rupert decide, even so, that he had a chance to win? In his pocket Rupert had the King's letter sanctioning a pitched battle, and their easy victories in Lancashire had given the men of his army enormous confidence. Moreover, the Parliamentary generals were said not to be on the best of terms.

Rupert had every reason to fight and win a battle. The King's cause was now dominant in the West. Victory outside York would get Lord Newcastle's army moving south, to play its part in the concerted pincer attack on London, which was the King's essential strategy.

For King Charles the capture of London, where the wealth, manpower, shipping, and armament industry of the Parliamentary cause were concentrated, would end the war and give him back his throne. And for Parliament, the war could be won only by effectively destroying the King's army. Therefore in the Civil War, pitched battles were decisive.

Their vivid and cruel drama tells us the inner truth about this war. When men on either side came face to face and fought to a finish, they displayed as in the heightened illumination of a lightning flash the real though fluctuating strength of King and Parliament, the true nature of the fighting men on both sides, and the strength of their will to win.

Word came to Prince Rupert that the Parliamentary armies, after scuttling away so fast from the walls of York, were drawn up in order on a broad open space called Marston Moor, three miles outside the city. Rupert decided that his great chance had come to beat the Roundheads in the field.

Lord Newcastle counselled delay, and Prince Rupert answered him, perhaps too abruptly, 'Nothing venture, nothing have.' He ordered the eccentric Marquess to start moving his men out of York and on to the moor by four o'clock next morning.

This peremptory command was perhaps a military necessity, but in human terms the Prince's tone of voice was ill judged. That brave aristocratic muddle-head, the Marquess of Newcastle, was unaccustomed to taking orders from anyone. It was doubtful anyway if his men would obey an order to get on the move that early, and certainly Lord Eythin, the Marquess's professional general, would do nothing to get them moving.

Years before, Lord Eythin had been a mercenary officer at the disastrous battle of Vlotho, in Germany, when young Rupert, then a colonel, had been taken prisoner. Eythin had saved his own skin by well-timed flight. He was chagrined now at having to serve under the orders of the gallant young prince he was generally held to have betrayed.

Early next day, 2 July 1644, Rupert's cavalry patrols brought him word that the enemy's generals appeared to have changed their minds. The allied armies were marching south.

Among the Roundheads, too, there had been differences of opinion. Fairfax was eager to give battle. Cromwell had done his best to stiffen Lord Manchester's apprehensive half-heartedness. But all the English were amateur generals. They listened with great respect to the opinions of paunchy little old Lord Leven, a real professional, chosen years ago by the King of Sweden – the Protestant hero – to be his field marshal.

Lord Leven had been a very distinguished soldier in his day, but he had the cunning of the man who fights for money. The Scottish government was being paid handsomely for the services of the army he commanded. Why smash it up in battle? Lord Leven lacked an urgent motive for victory. He urged prudence, and his argument sounded convincing.

Let the three armies quit Marston Moor, argued Leven, and march south-west. With Tadcaster as a base, they could cover the approaches to London. In the past, at Turnham Green and Newbury, a defensive strategy like this had served the Roundheads well. So far in this war they had never accepted battle until it was forced upon them.

At dawn, the Scots infantry headed the march towards Tadcaster. Soon all the roads south of York were filled with marching columns of pikemen and musketeers, miles long and vulnerable to cavalry attack. Prince Rupert's scouts reported from Marston Moor that this deliberate retreat was being covered by a rearguard of 3,000 cavalry and dragoons.

John Lilburne, the young hero of the London apprentice lads, had long since been freed from his royal prison in Oxford. Promoted lieutenant-colonel, Freeborn John, as he was nicknamed, was now commanding Oliver Cromwell's dragoons. On horseback that morning in his scarlet coat at the head of his men, John Lilburne had the prime task of keeping watch on the approaching Cavaliers. Fairfax, Cromwell, and the Scots cavalry leader Sir David Leslie were commanding the cavalry rearguard.

None of the Cavaliers bothered to move out of York until

nine, five hours later than Prince Rupert had ordered, but by now John Lilburne could see a mass of them riding by troop and regiment from the walled city towards Marston Moor – a huge field, planted half in rye, half lying waste.

Were those Cavaliers coming out to offer battle, or merely preparing to harass Lord Leven's columns of dusty, thirsty footsoldiers on their way to Tadcaster?

Shortly after nine, John Lilburne saw the Marquess of Newcastle himself arrive on the field in a gilded six-horse coach, followed by his troop of gentlemen volunteers. Prince Rúpert, huge on his black charger, was there already, and rode up to the coach. The generals doffed hats, and Rupert remarked to Newcastle 'My Lord, I wish you had come sooner with your forces – but I hope we shall yet have a glorious day.'

Though considered by professional soldiers to be only an amateur at the art of war, Sir Thomas Fairfax had the greatest gift a general can possess – the uncanny knack of guessing with total accuracy what was in his enemy's mind. Looking across Marston Moor at the random comings and goings of the Cavaliers, Fairfax decided before anyone else that Prince Rupert meant to offer battle. Fairfax, on his own responsibility, sent gallopers urgently down all the roads that led to Tadcaster to ask every allied commander to turn about smartly and bring his troops back to the field.

Slowly, through that long, hot, oppressive summer morning, John Lilburne saw the dilatory Royalists march out from their camp at York. Prince Rupert formed his army into a two-mile arc of armed men, horse and foot, at the northern side of Marston Moor. To the south, on the Parliament side, the Scots, all dusty and thirsty, were the first to get back. They were told that the field sign today would be a patch of white paper or rag worn on hat or helmet, and Fairfax indicated to them their place on the battlefield.

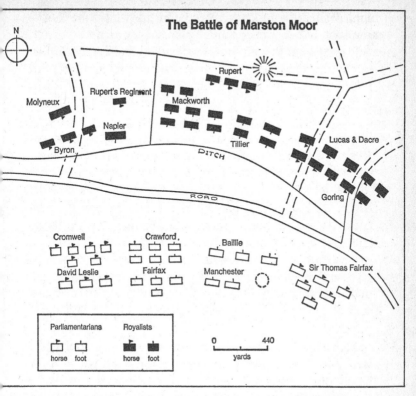

How the two armies were drawn up on Marston Moor, ready to give battle, on 2 July 1644

The gap between the waiting armies was about four hundred yards – a musket ball could just carry across. From a safe distance, a growing crowd of country folk watched as the armies formed up to give battle.

There was plenty of time for Rupert to arrange his troops in formation for the kind of set-piece battlefield he had studied so intently as a boy-prisoner in the Imperial fortress. For his front line he chose the hedge and ditch separating the wild part of the moor from the ryefield, which the Parliamentary soldiers were trampling flat as they arrived.

Rupert's battle plan looked splendidly correct, according to the military science of the time, but at 4 p.m., when Lord Eythin at last arrived and was shown it, he exploded sarcastically 'By God, sir, it is very fine on paper, but there is no such thing in the field.' Eythin pointed out – correctly, for with all his faults he was an expert professional – that Rupert had drawn up the royal army too close to the enemy. That ditch would not be a protection but a handicap.

The twenty-five-year-old Prince, about to fight his first battle, then suggested that he might perhaps pull his men back, but the veteran Eythin warned him 'No, sir, it is too late.' Across the moor, Fairfax's cavalry were poised to strike. Half an hour later, as Prince Rupert began to show his usual impatience, Lord Eythin again managed to get under his skin, reminding him insolently 'Sir, your forwardness lost us the day in Germany, where yourself was taken prisoner.'

Mercenary soldiers, in these armies led by amateurs, had a war aim of their own. The German wars had gone on for nearly thirty years, the war in the Low Countries for twice as long. The longer a war lasted, the better a mercenary soldier's chances of pay and promotion. A private joke among mercenaries in England in 1644 was 'This war, well managed, will last twenty years.'

All that long summer afternoon both sides waited within musket shot of each other. As usual, the footsoldiers occupied the centre of the battle-line, their blocks of high pikes bristling like steel forests, with musketeers in the gaps between. On the wings to left and right, cavalry chafed and curvetted, or cropped the trampled rye. The men were so thirsty that all the ponds on Marston Moor had already been drunk dry.

Halfway through the afternoon the field guns opened up – light guns throwing a three-pound ball. They coughed noisily at each other for an hour without doing much damage, then fell quiet. The sun was hot, the day humid. Here, confronting each other hour after hour, and waiting arms in hand, were representative Englishmen whose deep political and religious disagreements had somehow made them mortal enemies. Yet the differences between them were real.

Lord George Goring, who led that mass of impatient horsemen on the Cavaliers' left, was the son of the peer – now called Lord Norwich – whose percentages on butter and sugar had so embittered the hard-working Londoners. George Goring himself had already earned a bad name as a plunderer and debauchee – as if he had inherited his father's greed, but gave it expression in another way.

The stern cavalry halted on the Parliamentary left was led by Cromwell, a man who before the war had earned £300 a year as a working farmer. In earnest preparation for the testing time of battle, Oliver Cromwell had spent a long time alone, with an open Bible in front of him, deep in prayer. His dragoon commander was cheerful, witty John Lilburne, whose back was still scarred from King Charles's whip.

Over the way from John Lilburne, sitting superbly astride his bloodstock charger, was that accomplished horseman and fabulously rich landowner, the Marquess of Newcastle, living out to the very last his private dream of a more ample, gracious, and poetic age. Newcastle's relations with his tenants were fatherly, almost feudal. Those loyal Whitecoats in the ranks of the royal infantry were ready to fight to their last drop of blood for the Marquess and the King.

Prince Rupert was a romantic and honourable soldier, who had trained and fought since the age of thirteen in the hope of recovering his mother's kingdom, as now at the age of twenty-five he was fighting to save his uncle's.

He now sensed that the decisive historical clash had come. Much had been told of Oliver Cromwell and his new cavalry. A prisoner admitted that the cavalry leader directly opposite the Prince was the notorious Cromwell himself. 'And will they fight?' asked Rupert, who had never yet seen Roundhead cavalry that would stand up to him. 'If they will, they shall have fight enough.'

The Lowland Scots, all devout Presbyterians, sang metrical psalms as they stood waiting in their ranks on Marston Moor; the Cavaliers shook dice. About six that evening, Lord Newcastle asked Rupert if he intended to attack the enemy that same night. Prince Rupert, taking it for granted that the Roundheads would always act on the defensive, answered that he would charge them in the morning.

Rupert then let his men break ranks to eat their bread and cheese, and he went off to share a supper with his white poodle, Boy. Lord Newcastle himself dined snugly inside his opulent, booklined, six-horse coach and was smoking a long clay pipe to aid his digestion when, at about half past seven, the long summer day broke in a thunderstorm, with a downpour of rain and hail.

As the rain came down and the heavens shook, shrewd old Lord Leven from his post in the Parliamentary centre gave the signal for attack.

As if the first clap of thunder had been a sign from on high, the entire allied line went forward towards the Royalist enemy. The musketeers' rolling fire and the hammering hooves of the cavalry's chargers as they clattered forward outdid the thunder. An eyewitness declared that they came against their Royalist foe with 'such a noise, with shot and clamour of shouts, that we lost our ears, and the smoke of powder was so thick that we saw no light than what proceeded from the mouths of guns.'

Prince Rupert's front-line cavalry, on the wing facing

Oliver Cromwell, was commanded by Lord Byron, the officer who had led his Oxford student volunteers in such a hotheaded charge at Edgehill. In typical Cavalier fashion Byron now led his riders headlong with raised swords straight at Oliver Cromwell's Ironsides. Cromwell's men had leaped the ditch and were coming towards them through the pelting hail at a sober trot. Prince Rupert had placed squads of Royalist musketeers to rake Cromwell's men as they moved forward, but Byron's impetuous charge masked this fire.

The troopers fell upon each other mercilessly – gentlemen's sons who believed in precedence hacking for all they were worth at yeomen's sons with swords in their hands who yearned for equality. But for once, the yeomen's sons were standing their ground and hacking back. Lord Byron's Cavaliers began to shift and give way.

This was more than Prince Rupert could stand by and see happen. Though his duty, as commanding general, was to stay in the rear and give battlefield orders, he spurred his great black charger forward. Up at the head of his own lifeguards came Rupert to sustain Byron's charge, roaring like an inspired maniac at Cavaliers who had dared to give ground 'Swounds! Do you run? Follow me!' Rupert himself fought hand to hand in the thickest of the fray.

'Cromwell's own division had a hard pull of it,' reported Leonard Watson, who led the Roundhead scouts. 'For they were charged by Rupert's bravest men both in front and flank. They stood at sword's point a pretty while, hacking one another, but at last (it so pleased God) he broke through them, scattering them before him like a little dust.'

For the first time in the war, the best Parliamentary cavalry was beating the King's best troopers in a fair fight. Cromwell's Ironsides – a nickname given them by Rupert – now demonstrated the quality that made them different from all others: their almost inhuman puritanical discipline. Instead of galloping headlong in pursuit of their defeated enemy, they reined in grimly and waited for the next word of command.

To the right of Cromwell's horse, the Parliamentary foot, led by Lord Manchester, had come on bravely through the thunderstorm at the run. They crossed the ditch and slowly pressed the Royalist infantry back. Some of the royal foot-soldiers had not long since been levied by Rupert in Lancashire. They now threw down their arms, shouting loudly to the advancing Roundheads that they were pressed men and had no heart in this fight.

But once Manchester's foot came up against Lord Newcastle's famous Northumbrians, in their undyed white coats, their forward march was checked.

The crisis of the battle occurred on the far wing, where Fairfax commanded. Once in action, Black Tom Fairfax was a transformed man, no longer shy and courteous but a reckless devil of wild courage. Headlong over hedge and ditch he led his own cavalry, to arrive at last amid the foe with only four hundred horsemen still at his back. But to Fairfax in this mood, four hundred men were enough.

Tom Fairfax led his four hundred in a whirlwind charge at Goring's horse. The Cavaliers' extreme left wing broke on impact, and Fairfax's handful gave chase, but their flank as they rode past was exposed to the terrible musketry of Newcastle's Whitecoats. That fusillade destroyed them.

Black Tom himself was left there on the battlefield, alone, surrounded by enemy horsemen, his cheek gashed open by a sword cut, and all his officers dead.

Sir Thomas Fairfax had never in his life cropped his pate, Roundhead fashion. His long hair and his presence of mind now saved his life. Left alone and wounded amid the Cavalier foe, he shook out his black ringlets and took the giveaway patch of white paper from his helmet. Calmly, no different in

a and b. John Pym — nicknamed 'King Pym'— who organized the opposition to King Charles I in the House of Commons, and John Hampden, another of the five members accused of treason by the King *(British Museum and Radio Times Hulton Picture Library)*

c. King Charles I hoped to take the Five Members by surprise and arrest them in the House of Commons. But all the birds had flown *(British Museum)*

The Royalists
a. Charles I with his
beloved Queen, Henrietta
Maria *(John Freeman)*
b. The dashing Prince
Rupert, the King's nephew,
who led the Royalist
cavalry *(National Portrait
Gallery)*

The Puritans
c. Oliver Cromwell in full
armour. A page is tying his
sash *(National Portrait
Gallery)*
d. Black Tom Fairfax, the
young general who led the
New Model Army to
victory *(British Museum)*
e. John Lilburne was one
of Cromwell's bravest
commanders and a great
fighter for the freedom of
the individual. He later
became a passionate critic
of the Commonwealth
Parliament, and was exiled
in 1652 *(Radio Times
Hulton Picture Library)*

A buffcoat and bandolier. It was easier
to load a pistol or carbine with the
cartridges dangling from the bandolier
than with a powder horn *(London
Museum)*

A triple-barred helmet of the type worn
by Cromwell's army *(London Museum)*

Pikemen were specially selected, and
were much stronger than the musketeers.
They often wore helmets and breastplates
to protect them when it came 'to push of
pike' *(London Museum)*

Top: Cavaliers eat their supper clustered around the Marquess of Newcastle's coach just before the battle opens on Marston Moor *(Radio Times Hulton Picture Library)*

Bottom: An artist's impression of the battle for Prince Rupert's standard at Marston Moor, which ended in a stunning Puritan victory *(National Army Museum)*

Top left: Archibald Campbell - first Marquess of Argyll and Montrose's implacable enemy *(National Portrait Gallery)*

Top right: James Graham - first Marquess of Montrose, poet, scholar, soldier and King Charles's Lieutenant-General for Scotland *(National Galleries of Scotland)*

Bottom: Henry Ireton. He led the Ironside right wing at Naseby, and married Cromwell's daughter Bridget *(National Portrait Gallery)*

Cheshire gentlemen who fought for King Charles at the siege of Leicester - their weapons, costume and the fife and drum that led them into battle *(Grosvenor Museum, Chester)*

Top: The death warrant of 'Charles Stuart King of England' with the signatures of the commissioners who condemned him, headed by Bradshaw, president of the court *(British Museum)*

Bottom: 30 January, 1649 - 'Behold the head of a traitor'. The masked executioner holds up King Charles's severed head while soldiers of the New Model Army keep the London crowd at a safe distance *(John Freeman)*

Eleven years after his father's execution the Prince of Wales
returned to England as King Charles II *(National Portrait
Gallery)*

his appearance from any other bloodstained Cavalier trotting away in mid-battle to get his wound dressed, he rode through the encircling enemy to the rear.

Fairfax rode the length of the battlefield behind his enemies' backs. He managed at last to reach Cromwell's disciplined and victorious horsemen drawn up on the far side. The Ironsides were ready to strike once more and were only too glad to follow Black Tom Fairfax's inspired lead. But by this time they were the last Roundhead troops on Marston Moor still in good order.

George Goring had kept the bulk of his Royalist cavalry in hand. He led them across the ditch, to charge Fairfax's reserve, a green, untrained second line of horsemen who galloped away in desperate flight, spreading panic through all Lord Leven's men in the rear. The chase went on until Goring's horsemen reached the Parliamentary baggage train, where the Cavaliers reined in their foaming chargers and began happily to plunder.

A crow flying at that moment across the battlefield would have seen that victory was visibly going to the Royalists. In the centre, Puritan Lord Manchester's foot had failed to hold the ground they had won with their first rush. The terrible Northumbrian Whitecoats came forward at them on the run with lowered pikes, and the Roundhead infantry were pushed back to join the chaotic tangle of horses and men at their own rear. Lord Manchester's chaplain, Simeon Ashe, saw at that moment 'many thousands posting away, amazed with panic fears.'

The centre, which little old Lord Leven had commanded, was the point of greatest confusion. Lord Leven made up his mind that the battle was lost. Short and paunchy, clumsy on horseback, Leven was lifted into the saddle by his aides, and did not cease spurring his charger's flanks until he had reached the city of Leeds, twenty miles away.

The famous general was seen in full flight, and news of a Royalist victory ran ahead of him. Church-bells were rung in village after village, until the good word reached Oxford, where bonfires of triumph were lighted in the streets.

In that long midsummer twilight, the battlefield of Marston Moor had become like a chessboard towards the end of a hard-fought game, when most of the more powerful chessmen on both sides have been captured. But on the almost empty board still lurked one powerful piece, the Queen of the battlefield – Oliver Cromwell's disciplined Puritan cavalry. Black Tom Fairfax had trotted them around in good order to the rear of the triumphant Royalist army, where a sudden charge would have the most demoralizing effect.

'And here came the business of the day,' wrote Sir Thomas Fairfax afterwards, 'nay, almost of the kingdom, to be disputed upon this second charge. The enemy, seeing us come up in such a gallant posture to charge them, left all thoughts of pursuit, and began to think that they must fight again for that victory which they thought had been already got.'

There was one Royalist cavalry formation still on the field, led here as at Edgehill by cool-headed, intrepid Sir Charles Lucas. Trotting in line after Fairfax and Cromwell, both of them wounded earlier in the fight, the troopers from East Anglia rode with lifted swords up the slope of the field against Lucas's Cavaliers – and drove them headlong from the Moor.

That left only one group of King's men still in fighting formation, the famous Whitecoats. These Northumbrians had marched up late to the fight, muttering superstitiously among themselves of having 'brought their winding sheets into the field.' Now they had to face the onslaught of the Ironsides. Retreating step by step, these tough soldiers took cover in a dry stone-walled enclosure called White Sike Close, and there they made a memorable last stand.

Their pikes behind the stone wall were like an unbreakable shifting wall of steel blades. The Ironsides charged again and again, yet could not break their ranks. At last Cromwell ordered John Lilburne to dismount his dragoons. Lilburne led his men on foot against the ranks of the Royalist White-coats, ducking under their pike blades to fight recklessly hand to hand with the sword until a gap had been forced in the Whitecoat line wide enough for the Ironsides to shoulder their horses through and lay about them.

The Whitecoat musketeers had long ago fired off all their shot. Against the mounted swordsmen they fought back on foot with clubbed musket. Whitecoats lay wounded in the ground and struck upwards with their last gasp at the riders trampling over them. This death grapple between Whitecoats and Ironsides went on until long after dark. Of the entire Whitecoat regiment, only thirty were taken alive.

Cromwell at last unleashed his Puritan troopers, and their mood changed from iron discipline to passionate cruelty. Roundhead cavalry thundered across the field after defeated Royalists, cutting them down left and right like helpless animals.

Sir Thomas Fairfax, gentle and considerate once the cut-and-thrust was over, went to and fro on horseback across the Moor, trying to save the lives of the Royalist Englishmen who were being wantonly slaughtered. His high voice could be heard in the night exclaiming 'Spare the poor deluded countrymen, ah, spare them, I pray, who are deluded, and know not what they do.' He could command obedience in battle, but not forbid this cold-blooded slaughter.

Oliver Cromwell was out to destroy the King's army. The three-mile road to York was lined with the slain. The streets of York were choked with screaming men left untended in rows in the open air. Of King Charles's men, 4,150 were killed, of the Parliamentarians, about 300.

There was nothing to eat for the victors on Marston Moor that night because their baggage had been plundered. After the killing was over, the bloodstained and hungry Roundhead army joined together with the Scots in singing King David's psalm of victory. Towards midnight, as his bone-weary soldiers began dropping asleep on the ground amid the unburied dead, Lord Manchester went earnestly among them, from group to group, urging them to honour God for the victory, and promising them food in the morning.

The Marquess of Newcastle – a brave if fantastic gentleman – had fought in the thick of the battle as a mere captain at the head of his troop of volunteers. When the Whitecoats – Lord Newcastle's tenants, and many of them Roman Catholic – died for his cause on Marston Moor to the last handful of men, that sort of old-fashioned, staunch local loyalty went to its death in England. Something new and different, something as mechanical and remorseless as Ironside discipline, had begun to take its place.

Prince Rupert managed to save his neck by ducking down and hiding in a beanfield until the heat of pursuit was over. He then cut his way to York and tried to rally those of his men who still had the spirit to fight on. Meeting Lord Newcastle late on that disastrous night, the Prince was unable to persuade the rich and aristocratic eccentric to follow him. 'No,' declared the Marquess, 'I will not endure the laughter of the Court.' Lord Newcastle rode to Scarborough,

---

Some of the Roundheads believed that Prince Rupert's poodle, Boy, who followed him into battle, must be an evil spirit – and this pamphlet sardonically celebrates Boy's death at Marston Moor. Ferdinando, Lord Fairfax, was Black Tom Fairfax's father, who commanded some of the rearward infantry at Marston Moor but lacked his son's valour and genius (British Library)

A
DOGS ELEGY,
OR
RVPERT'S TEARS,

For the late Defeat given him at *Marston-moore*, neer *York*, by the Three Renowned Generalls; *Alexander Earl of* Leven, *Generall of the Scottiſh Forces,* Fardinando *Lord* Fairefax, *and the Earle of* Man-cheſter *Generalls of the* Engliſh *Forces in the North*.

Where his beloved Dog, named *B O Y*, was killed by a Val-liant Souldier, who had skill in *Necromancy*.

Likewiſe the ſtrange breed of this Shagg'd Cavalier, whelp'd of a Malignant Water-witch; With all his Tricks, and Feats.

Sad Cavaliers, *Rupert* invites you all   Cloſe-mourners are the Witch, Pope, & devill,
That doe ſurvive, to his Dogs Funerall.   That much lament your late befallen evill.

Printed at *London*, for *G. B.* July 27. 1644.

and there hired a fishing smack to carry him to exile in Hamburg.

Prince Rupert managed to gather up 6,000 survivors, and the next day he led them out of York in good order. There was no pursuit. Downcast at his defeat, Rupert lingered on for two months in Lancashire and Cheshire at the scene of his easy victories, drinking heavily, unable to face the King, his uncle, whose cause the destruction of an entire royal army at Marston Moor had put in grave jeopardy. Even Rupert's white poodle Boy, claimed by Puritans to be his evil spirit, was dead. The dog had run after him from the supper table to the battlefield, and had there been killed.

On 16 July 1644, the city of York, the King's capital in the north of England, formally surrendered to Parliament. Sir Thomas Fairfax brought all his influence to bear on the terms of surrender. York was a city he loved, and whatever else happened, he intended to save the stained glass in the Minster from the brickbats of Puritan bigots. Being an obstinate Yorkshireman, he succeeded, and thanks to him the last of England's once magnificent stained glass can still be seen in York Minster.

CHAPTER EIGHT

Jesus – and No Quarter!

There are three things I will not part with – the Church, my crown, and my friends; and you will have much ado to get them from me – KING CHARLES I to a Parliamentary Commission sent to Oxford to discuss peace (1644)

> He either fears his fate too much,
>   Or his deserts are small,
> Who dares not put it to the touch,
>   And win or lose it all.
> – JAMES GRAHAM, Marquess of Montrose

THE stunning Puritan triumph at Marston Moor destroyed the King's army in the north and left him only the army centred at Oxford and Bristol. But on the Roundhead side the effect of the victory was dissipated, for some were beginning to doubt in their hearts that they ever wanted to defeat King Charles totally.

After the battle, Lord Leven and his Scots hung about York for five idle weeks, though the capture of the Tyneside coal ports was both easy and urgent. About this time Sir William Waller admitted frankly 'I am so heartily weary of this war that I shall submit to anything that may conduce to the dispatch of it.' The Earl of Essex was gnawed by the thought that his own side might mistrust him, and he started to act with a foolish rashness to prove his own courage.

As for Lord Manchester, he commanded a victorious army but was unwilling to let it fight. When John Lilburne asked for permission to march his dragoons against Tickhill Castle, where an easy success could be won, Manchester shouted at him 'Get thee gone, thou art a mad fellow!'

John Lilburne decided to pretend that this answer must be his lordship's individual way of saying 'Yes'. Lilburne's dragoons captured Tickhill Castle and all its garrison without firing a shot, but for this good day's work all John Lilburne got was a sharp dressing-down.

The rich Puritans who had been the first to go to war were now frightened of the prospect of victory.

Queen Henrietta Maria – fervent for the royal cause – had recently been impeached by Parliament, which meant that, if captured, she would go to the scaffold. This threat to the wife he dearly loved was supposed to change King Charles's obstinate mind about giving up his powers to Parliament.

The Queen was expecting a baby. She asked Lord Essex for a safe conduct from Oxford to Bath, for the sake of her health. Essex refused, though he offered 'to take her to London, where the best medical advice was to be had.' This was a joke in poor taste, since in London nothing awaited the Queen of England except the headsman's axe. So in April 1644, Henrietta Maria, though very unwell, set off boldly across country to Exeter, a Royalist stronghold in the west.

The Queen was brought to bed there in June of a little princess, the prettiest of her children, who was christened Henrietta. But hardly was her confinement over than Essex marched his army towards Exeter. The Queen, in great pain, was compelled to leave her baby with a nurse and scamper as fast as she could to loyal Cornwall. On 14 July, in Falmouth, she found a Dutch ship called *George* willing to take her across the Channel to France.

But William Batten was lurking in the Channel off Falmouth. He was the Parliamentary vice-admiral who, twenty months earlier, on the snowy night she landed at Bridlington, had welcomed the Queen with a bombardment. This time there were three ships-of-war in Batten's squadron –

Reformation, *Paragon*, and *Warwick*. As the Dutchman *George*, with the sick Queen on board, came out of Falmouth into the teeth of a sou'westerly gale, Batten fired ten shots at her from the 44-gun *Reformation*. But the Dutch captain, a fine seaman, managed to claw offshore and got to windward of the big warship, so they could try to make a run for it.

The more manoeuvrable 22-gun *Warwick* moved up to exchange shots with *George*, and for safety the Queen was sent down into the hold. With a flash of her old audacity she sent a message to the Dutch captain ordering him to blow up his ship rather than let her be caught.

The running gunfight between *George* and the three warships went on all the way across the Channel. Off Jersey, *George* was badly hit in the rigging, but before Batten could close in and take the Queen prisoner, some ships from Dieppe in France came in sight. Mistaking them for a French escort, Batten sheered off. The Queen got safely ashore in Brittany, but she was never to see her husband again.

As long as a month before Henrietta Maria's escape to France, Essex had received a letter from his superiors in London, recalling him from the west. Yet he decided to ignore this order and march on westward after the Queen.

An old friend of his called Lord Robartes had privately assured Lord Essex that the West Country was Parliamentarian at heart, but held down against its will by an army of Cavaliers. Essex saw this as his great chance. Fairfax and Cromwell had won a spectacular victory – he might win another.

Lord Essex, as he moved west in pursuit of the sick Queen, did not know that King Charles had broken out of Worcester with an army twice as big as his own. After a sharp little victory at Cropredy Bridge over the Roundheads who were supposed to be keeping him bottled up, the King headed westward too. Essex, as he followed in the Queen's track towards the peninsula of Cornwall, was marching his ten thousand men into the far end of a long, dark sack.

At the River Tamar, dividing Devon from Cornwall, Lord Essex still had a chance to obey orders, turn back, and perhaps regain London without fighting a battle. But once again he listened to Lord Robartes, an immensely rich Cornish Puritan, who had made his money out of tin-mining and increased it by money-lending. Lord Robartes was another of the rich men who had bought his peerage for £10,000 cash down. Robartes badly wanted to get back to his great mansion in Cornwall, so his advice to Essex to cross the Tamar was tainted with self-interest.

Essex entered Cornwall with his army, but by the time he had reached Bodmin, the countryside that was supposed to welcome him as a deliverer had risen in arms against him. And by 26 July, King Charles and his army of 16,000 men reached Exeter.

Charles had taken personal command. The black news of Rupert's defeat at Marston Moor was already known to the King. But with boldness the West might yet be saved. In the coming weeks King Charles, whose personal courage had never been questioned, was to prove himself also a reliable general.

On 1 August, Charles followed Essex across the Tamar, breaking all the bridges behind him. He now had Essex and his 10,000 Roundheads cooped up in Cornwall, with no way home except by sea. Essex's last hope was that Lord Warwick, who commanded Parliament's navy, might somehow sail down-Channel and take all his men off in the ships. Essex therefore moved his army towards the Cornish port of Fowey.

But King Charles came down on Lord Essex much faster than Parliament's fleet could sail up. The wind was blowing so strong and persistent a gale from the south-west that no sailing ship could make headway. 'God hath not for many days past,' wrote Warwick to Essex in despair, 'given us wind serviceable.'

On 31 August, the Roundhead cavalry made a bold night's march through the King's lines and fought its way back to Plymouth. The sou'westerly wind prevented warships from coming down-Channel to rescue the army, but the same wind enabled Lord Essex and Lord Robartes to escape out of Fowey in a local fishing boat and sail at a spanking pace up-Channel to safety at Plymouth. Loyal old Philip Skippon was left behind at Lostwithiel to manage the surrender of the 6,000 infantry.

King Charles, who led his troops in person, had slept the night before under a hedge in a gale. His terms of surrender to Skippon on 2 September were generous. The Roundhead infantry gave up their arms and were allowed to march away to their friends in Plymouth, 'pressed all of a heap, like sheep,' said an eyewitness, 'but not so innocent.' And the King and his officers rode up and down the marching column to hold back the Royalist rank and file from plundering.

But the country people could not be restrained. They had learned by now to hate the sight of all soldiers, whatever side they were on, and on the march back to Plymouth they stripped the helpless Roundheads down to their last rags. Only 4,000 of Skippon's men reached Plymouth alive.

Could these demoralized survivors of Lord Essex's army – or Waller's defeated troops – be any longer relied upon to defend the western approaches to London? Oliver Cromwell's opinions might be mistrusted by the rich Presbyterians who now controlled Parliament, but at least his men had proved that they knew how to fight.

Parliament in this extremity ordered the formation of a

New Model Army (or 'New Noddle Army' as the Cavaliers mockingly called it), incorporating all the best of the troops that were still left, to be trained and led in the same way as the East Anglian troops who fought with such effect at Marston Moor.

As he led his defeated Cavaliers away from Marston Moor, Rupert paused at Richmond in Yorkshire. In a tavern there he had conferred with a slightly built, scholarly aristocrat of thirty-two, the Marquess of Montrose, who said to the Prince coolly 'Give me a thousand of your horse, and I will cut my way into the heart of Scotland.' But Rupert at that moment had little time to waste on incorrigible Scottish optimists, and he certainly had no cavalry to spare.

Scotland, with only a million inhabitants, had almost no trade or industry. The English-speaking Lowlanders were stoutly Presbyterian, but many of the Gaelic-speaking Highlanders were still Roman Catholic and would certainly fight for King Charles. Suppose the Highlanders were to put up such a good fight that Lord Leven's army had to be brought back to Scotland? The King might even regain the north.

Montrose knew that the Highlanders were wildly undisciplined and fought for pride and plunder. They needed a stiffening of trained soldiers, and Rupert had no such men to spare. But unknown to Montrose, the veteran troops he needed were already on their way – from Ireland.

Lord Antrim's grandfather, a Catholic and a chieftain of Clan MacDonald, had emigrated to Ireland with all his retainers in Queen Elizabeth's day. After he left Scotland, the Campbells slowly drove MacDonald clansmen from their ancestral lands in the Highlands and Islands. Now the Irish MacDonalds – Roman Catholic and Gaelic-speaking – having helped to win the war in Ireland against the English, were coming home again to aid their Scottish cousins against the clan's enemy, the Marquess of Argyll.

Red-haired, cross-eyed, tight-mouthed Archibald Campbell, the forty-year-old Marquess of Argyll and chief of Clan Campbell, was the dominating personality among the Presbyterians in Scotland. A Cavalier historian once said of Argyll that he 'wanted nothing but honesty and courage to be a very extraordinary man.' The Highlands elsewhere might still be Roman Catholic, but in Argyll's Highland domains, Presbyterian ministers preached and taught freely. Argyll was dragging Clan Campbell headlong into the modern world.

Argyll used his influence in the church with ruthless single-mindedness. Under his unloved and sombre shadow, denunciations for witchcraft were commonplace. Covenanting ministers took to interfering to a ludicrous extent in the lives of ordinary believers, forbidding them, for instance, to give Christmas presents, and making country people do penance for watering their cabbages on the Sabbath. Any Scot of independent mind was in those days at the mercy of an informer.

The Marquess of Montrose himself was a Presbyterian born and bred, but, as a well-read and warm-hearted gentleman, he detested the cheerless way of life that Argyll's church had managed to impose upon his fellow-countrymen. Montrose believed that his Lowland neighbours were 'either fooled or forced' into their total obedience to the Covenanting church. He was probably mistaken. Some may have found Presbyterian discipline too systematic to escape, but most thinking men gave their consent to it, as Scotland's best guarantee against being swallowed up by England. The Highlands might rise for Montrose. Would the Lowlands reject him?

*

On 18 August 1644, two Scottish gentlemen, lame Sir William Rollo and his friend Colonel Sibbald, set off northwards from Carlisle in disguise. They were dressed as a couple of Lord Leven's troopers going home on leave after Marston Moor, but they travelled chiefly by night. Behind them, leading a spare horse, rode a shabby groom. Into the lining of his saddle the groom – Montrose – had sewn the broad parchment of his commission as King Charles's Lieutenant-General for Scotland.

Montrose in his shabby garb had as yet no troops at his back, just two loyal comrades, and a private conviction that the Highlands could be roused to fight for King Charles. After four days' hard riding he led his friends to Tullibelton near Perth, the house of a kinsman, Patrick Graham.

Rollo and Sibbald went off to scour the countryside for news. Most of it was bad. Half-hearted Royalists were wavering, some of them going over to the Covenanters to save their lands. But after six days' wait, a letter reached Tullibelton after passing from hand to hand, and it brought Montrose good news.

Antrim's Irish had landed two months earlier. After marching the breadth of Scotland only to find the King's cause everywhere at a low ebb of defeat, they were now at a loss what to do. They needed the King's Lieutenant-General to give them a lead.

This letter was from their leader, Alasdair MacDonald, son of MacDonald of Colonsay, an enemy whom Argyll had for years kept locked up in one of his dungeons. Alasdair, a fearless young giant of twenty-five, stood six feet six in his brogues. He was sometimes a little too fond of the bottle, but he was staunch in his faith, never eating meat without first hearing a Latin grace, never going into battle without receiving the sacrament. Lord Antrim had sent him over from Ireland with three veteran regiments of foot.

All 1,600 of Alasdair's soldiers had already fought well in the war in Ireland against the Protestant English. A quarter were English or Scottish Roman Catholics of families settled in Ireland. The rest, native Irish, had brought their wives and children and even their cattle with them, like a tribe on the march. Each regiment had a priest for chaplain. They had no cavalry, and there were very many more dirks, bows, and claymores among them than muskets.

In the past six weeks Alasdair had also managed to recruit five hundred Highlanders to the royal cause, but the Marquess of Argyll was now sending armies on his track, and Alasdair well knew he was no general. His two thousand men were simply waiting up in the hills for a leader. They had their camp at Blair.

Montrose walked twenty miles over the heather to the rendezvous. He was dressed in trews and a short coat and had a plaid across his shoulder. He wore a blue bonnet with a bunch of oats for a badge, and he was armed, Highland fashion, with broadsword and buckler. When Alasdair's musketeers caught sight of the King's general – not a pompous figure on horseback, but a slim, smiling, confident young man, dressed and armed like themselves – they blazed away the last of their gunpowder in a wild greeting.

On a green knoll nearby, Montrose unfurled the Royal Standard: in the first and fourth quarters, the Red Lion rampant of Scotland; in the second, the quartered Lilies and Lions of France and England; and the Harp of Ireland in the third. At last King Charles had an army in Scotland, an army with hardly any gunpowder, no pikes to hold off a mounted attack, and a cavalry force numbering three horses – the fourth horse, which Montrose had led up from Carlisle, having gone lame. His men had no cannon, no wagons, no supplies, and no money. They had nothing much else but their courage.

And this time, three fully organized enemy armies were on the move against them. In the west, Argyll was raising the fighting men of Clan Campbell. A second army, under Lord Burleigh, waited at Aberdeen, to bar Montrose's way into Gordon country – since the Gordons were Royalists. A third, of 7,000, under Lord Elcho, was at Perth – much too close for comfort. Montrose could see that his first task was to knock out Lord Elcho before Argyll arrived.

Lord Elcho's army at Perth outnumbered Montrose and his men by nearly three to one. Elcho had an irregular cavalry force of 700 – lairds and their mounted retainers. His army also boasted nine field-pieces, which the Highlanders spoke of in awe as 'the musket's mother' and which they disliked horribly. In the early hours of 1 September 1644, Lord Elcho drew up this well-furnished army in correct battle array – cavalry on the flanks, infantry in the centre – on Tippermuir, three miles outside Perth.

Elcho's men were, in fact, second-line troops, the best Covenanting infantry being over the border with Lord Leven. But they waited confidently for the outcome of a fight against a rabble of ill-armed Catholic Irish and wild Highlanders. As they stood in line upon the moor, Covenanting ministers moved up and down, reminding the inexperienced soldiers that God was on their side. The Reverend Frederick Carmichael went so far as to declare in a loud voice 'If ever God spake word of truth by my mouth, I promise you in His name certain victory today.' Lord Elcho gave them as their first battlecry 'Jesus – and no quarter!'

Montrose's handful of musketeers had only one cartridge apiece. In lieu of ammunition, he bade all his men fill their pockets with stones. Montrose intended to fight a quick and unnerving battle against this arrogantly confident foe. He drew his men out in a battle order that to the regular soldiers confronting him looked grotesque – a long line only three men deep, but a line so long it could not be outflanked. The best troops – the ragged and hungry Irish – took their posts in the centre of this line.

Montrose sent his kinsman, the Master of Maderty, as envoy across the green turf between the waiting armies to remind Lord Elcho formally that he was acting in the King's name on a royal commission, and sought above all to avoid shedding Scottish blood. Elcho, defying the usages of war, sent Maderty away prisoner, to be hanged once the battle was over.

The Covenanters moved forward a squadron of their cavalry. Their plan was to provoke the wild Highlanders into breaking their ranks by a premature charge. But Montrose's long triple line, instantly obeying the drumbeat of command, fired a volley at the horsemen – that is, some fired musket slugs, many more hurled stones. Wheeling in panic, the horses galloped back directly into Elcho's front line, bringing it to disorder. This was the moment when Montrose sounded the charge.

Against dirk and claymore and the blood-curdling Irish war-cries of Alasdair's veterans, Lord Elcho's God-fearing Presbyterian infantry turned tail and ran, his cavalry leading the way. Montrose lost scarcely a dozen men at Tippermuir, but 2,000 of Elcho's fugitives were slaughtered, even though Montrose managed to prevent his men from turning the nine captured cannon around and firing them into the backs of the retreating foe. An eyewitness later declared 'A man could have walked to Perth on the dead.'

Montrose imposed a strict discipline on his little army. He saved Perth from plunder but levied in return a contribution of cloth to make uniforms. Montrose's stone-throwing, barefoot troops had already armed themselves from the runaway enemy, and were soon clad and shod as an army should be.

On 4 September, Montrose led his men off for all to see in

the general direction of Dundee. But his real objective was
the second enemy army at Aberdeen. Though their women-
folk and children were marching along with them, his Irish
infantry averaged twenty miles a day. Argyll's mounted advance guard was six days' march behind. Montrose had to
reach Aberdeen and defeat the army there before Argyll
caught up with them.

Red-haired Argyll had already begun to show his true
nature. Since the King's army in Scotland was held together
by one man's commanding personality alone, to Argyll's bitter and dogmatic mind any way of destroying Montrose was
justified. In May, Montrose had been excommunicated by
the Kirk. Now a reward of £20,000 Scots (about £1,600
sterling) was offered, together with a free pardon for previous
crimes, to anyone who would assassinate Montrose and
bring his severed head to Edinburgh as proof.

The King's Lieutenant-General in Scotland was usually
scrupulous in observing the rules of war, but the sack of
Aberdeen was a sad lapse. He was moved to anger there by
an act of treachery, which an onlooker declared to have
'made Montrose mad'.

He sent a spokesman up to Aberdeen's city gate, carrying
a flag of truce, with the usual little drummer boy at his side,
whose sole duty was to beat a tattoo to gain attention. To
the Covenanters inside the city the envoy repeated a formal
warning from Montrose to send their women and children
to safety. Either they surrendered the city, he said, or he
would take it by assault. But as the messenger and drummer
boy turned their backs, a Covenanting musketeer shot the
boy dead. Montrose, in a moment of blind fury, promised to
let Alasdair and his men put the city to the sack.

Lord Balfour of Burleigh's Covenanting army, numbering
2,500, was drawn up on a sloping field outside the walls of

Aberdeen. The Marquess of Argyll had by this time left Perth behind him, and was lumbering on Montrose's track somewhere up in the mountains. Montrose was obliged to win quickly or else be caught between his two enemies.

Montrose had by now about 70 mounted troopers – younger sons of Royalist gentry, some of them Gordons – to oppose Burleigh's 500 horse. But Alasdair's men had a trick of their own against a cavalry charge, which they had used to good effect in Ireland.

When Burleigh threw the bulk of his cavalry against the Irish right flank, they made no attempt to fight back but opened their ranks to let horses and riders through. Then the Irish turned, aimed at the retreating backs of the cavalrymen, and knocked them out of the saddle with a volley of musketry. The survivors of Burleigh's cavalry rode in panic off the field.

The Irish then raised their voices in a chilling war-cry. Aware that all Aberdeen lay over there to be plundered, they flung themselves hectically at Burleigh's foot. The open space between hillside and city wall was soon a bloody shambles, and the Irish swept triumphantly over and through the city gates into Aberdeen.

The battle was fought on 13 September 1644. Inside Aberdeen the plunder and slaughter continued for another three days and nights. About a hundred of the better-dressed citizens were cut down in the streets and stripped naked, simply for the clothes they wore. No house was safe, and no woman either: As one of Alasdair's officers declared, 'The riches of that town hath made all our soldiers Cavaliers.'

Ministers in Presbyterian pulpits all over Scotland were soon warning their flocks about the sack of Aberdeen and exaggerating it to a blood-curdling orgy of brutal lust. Politically, it was certainly Montrose's first mistake. Many Aberdonians were King's men at heart, driven by fear of their neighbours to a hypocritical observance of Presbyterian ways. Scotland could be won for King Charles only if Montrose somehow gained the active support of such men, particularly in the Lowlands. But the sack of Aberdeen – as gaudily reported everywhere by the ministers – turned the waverers against him.

Montrose's winter quarters were at Blair Atholl. At Blair that winter the Irish soldiers lived domestically with their wives and children. Some lasses from Aberdeen – with names like Dunbar, Anderson, and Forbes – had gone off with Montrose's men after the sack of the city, probably not against their wills, and lived with them at Blair. Another five hundred Highlanders came in to join the camp – MacDonalds, Macleans, Stewarts of Appin, Camerons, all united in hatred of Clan Campbell. Until December, the winter of 1644 had not shown itself severe, but Argyll's Covenanters had little intention of fighting a winter campaign.

Montrose himself would have liked most to make a surprise march through the Lowlands and, by crossing the Border unexpectedly, put the fear of death into Lord Leven's army. But his Highlanders and his Irish alike were obsessed by the wrongs they had suffered in the past at the hands of Argyll and his clan. They pleaded with Montrose to lead them instead on a winter raid into Campbell country.

This too would be a blow, even if only an oblique one, struck in the royal cause. In a letter to King Charles, Montrose explained his motives for agreeing with his men. 'I was willing to let the world see Argyll was not the man his Highlanders believed him to be, and that it was possible to beat him in his own Highlands.'

The lands of Clan Campbell, some hereditary, but many wrested by force from their lesser neighbours, were a kingdom within a kingdom. The Campbells were by far the most numerous and prosperous clan in the Highlands – the only Highlanders who no longer lived from hand to mouth.

Their territory, rich with black cattle, was compact and easy to defend. One border faced the Lowlands, where, thanks to his influence in the Kirk, Argyll's political power was unquestioned. Another looked out to sea; Argyll not only owned many trading ships, but had a private navy. As chieftain, the Marquess of Argyll had despotic powers in Campbell country, and could put into the field an army of 5,000 clansmen obedient only to himself.

The Campbells' third border, to north and west – the direction from which Montrose planned to invade – ran through high mountains where the passes, always difficult, were usually blocked by snowdrifts in winter. Argyll had been heard to boast that his little capital city, Inveraray on Loch Fyne, was impregnable. But in this relatively mild winter, Montrose thought there might be a chance of getting through.

Montrose took three thousand men on the raid, marching them out of Blair Atholl in three divisions, the Irish under Alasdair, and the Highlanders under John of Moidart, Captain of Clanranald. Montrose himself commanded the small force of cavalry and the Royalist volunteers, some of whom had come to join the King's Lieutenant-General from as far away as Orkney. To feed all these men in the bleak mountains, Montrose sent Clanranald on ahead to forage.

The winter so far may have been mild by Scottish standards, but the march was appalling. Just as Montrose's raiders were beginning to feel the pinch of hunger, in came Clanranald and his Highlanders, joyfully driving before them a thousand head of Campbell cattle. Every Campbell cot and clachan they passed on their march had been set on fire. 'We left neither house nor hold unburned,' boasted one MacDonald, 'nor corn nor cattle that belonged to the whole name of Campbell.' But this cattle raid had given Argyll warning that his private kingdom was threatened.

All that winter Argyll, in his own vindictive fashion, had been carrying on the fight against Montrose. Any known friend or kinsman of Montrose's that Argyll could put his hand upon was already in prison. He intended also to confiscate the estates of Montrose, and to take away his rank and privileges as a nobleman.

Argyll was sure, however, that his little capital city of Inveraray was safe. Montrose would never get through the passes, and if he did, he would march into a trap. But to make doubly sure, Argyll rode post-haste across half Scotland, and he was there, in Inveraray, when wild-eyed shepherds ran into the streets to shout warning that Montrose and his army were up in the hills but a few miles off.

Argyll's nerve broke. To save his own skin, he sailed away down Loch Fyne in a fishing boat, leaving Inveraray to be plundered. This time the Highlanders were after loot, not blood, and they pillaged to their heart's content.

One of the regimental chaplains, a Jesuit popular with the army for his remarkable gift of foretelling the weather, then celebrated the first mass to be said in Campbell country for fifty years. A flat stone was placed on a pile of sheaves as an altar, and the devout Highlanders stood around in a ring, holding up their plaids as a screen against the wind. All the soldiers, Irish, Scots, and English, came in one by one and knelt to communicate. To Argyll, this was the final insult. Montrose had kept his promise to the King. The chief of Clan Campbell had been shown up as 'not the man his Highlanders believed him to be.'

Though lacking in personal courage, Argyll understood Highland warfare. He well knew that once the clansmen in Montrose's camp had plunder they would be unable to resist the temptation to drift off home with it. That was exactly what happened. Montrose's army dwindled away, and in the heart of hostile Campbell country he was soon left with only 1,500 fighting men.

Argyll was also well aware that somehow he must restore his reputation among his clansmen by a victory. As Montrose's little army tried to march out, Argyll intended to pursue them with the best of Leven's infantry – the veterans of Marston Moor. And should Montrose, who had already shown himself as hard to hold down as a bubble of quicksilver, somehow manage to move out too fast for Leven's men, Argyll had already seen to it that a second army, under George Mackenzie, Earl of Seaforth, would come down from Inverness and block the roads. This time there could be no possible way for Montrose to slip through Argyll's clutches.

As the retreating Royalist enemy briskly marched away northward from Inveraray by the coast road, Argyll sent an armed sloop from his private navy to bombard them. The sloop ran aground, leaving Montrose in possession of its handsome brass guns. By the evening of Wednesday, 29 January 1645, Montrose with his 1,500 men had marched so far as Cumin at the head of Loch Ness. Lord Seaforth's army, 5,000 strong, was up ahead only thirty-five miles away, barring the only road out.

Montrose had actually begun making his plans for an attack on Seaforth's 5,000 when Ian Lom MacDonald, the Bard of Keppoch, arrived breathlessly over the frozen hills with a warning that Argyll was even nearer than Montrose had suspected – at Inverlochy. And Argyll's army of 3,000 included the crack infantry sent him by Lord Leven. The two armies sent against Montrose were less than sixty miles apart, and they were closing on each other as fast as they could. This time they had Montrose trapped.

Argyll's scouts, riding one way, and Seaforth's scouts, riding the other down the only road out of Campbell country, met each other at Loch Ness. But the helplessly trapped little royal army, which they supposed to be somewhere in the shrinking gap between them, had disappeared.

Montrose had taken his men up into the freezing white hills, where usually no one dared travel in winter. Through snowdrifts and avalanches he was marching them back the way they had come, circling the high mountains around Ben Nevis parallel to the road up which Argyll's crack infantry were marching. He intended to take Argyll by surprise.

Most of Montrose's men on this journey through the mountains tasted no food for two days. They plodded knee-deep through snow and waded icy rivers 'up to their girdles'. Montrose dismounted and did the march on foot, so he would fare no better than his men.

At night, on the wooded hillside above Argyll's lochside castle of Inverlochy, Montrose's flankers brushed with outlying pickets of the enemy army. A few shots were exchanged, but Argyll was assured that Highlanders from some neighbouring clan must be firing potshots. The Covenanters had camped for the night near the castle on the shores of Loch Linnhe. Argyll had dislocated his shoulder in a fall from a horse, and had handed command over to his kinsman, Sir Duncan Campbell.

Sunday, 2 February, was Candlemas. The Irish celebrated communion before the sun came up, and the priests went in darkness down the lines of kneeling men, blessing their weapons. Across the hillside at the first glimmer of dawn, Montrose placed his 1,500 hungry men in battle order. As the sunlight glinted over the mountains, Argyll's sleeping infantrymen heard trumpeters from the hillside. They were sounding the Royal Salute. The Irish screamed their war-cry, the Cameron piper brayed out a spine-chilling pibroch, 'Sons of bitches, come, and I will give you flesh', and down the hill-side tumbled the Irish with their lifted broadswords.

Argyll watched them from the safety of his lymphad, a one-masted sailing galley, which was swinging at anchor out in the loch. The terrifying onset was enough for him. Not waiting to see the outcome of the battle, he hoisted sail and fled.

The crack Lowland infantry on the flanks broke and fled – the charge of George Goring's Cavaliers at Marston Moor had been nothing to this. The Campbells in the centre were left to take the brunt. 'Stout and gallant gentlemen,' admits Montrose's chronicler, 'worthy of a better chief and a juster cause.'

Montrose's handful of horsemen wheeled around cleverly to cut off their enemies' retreat to Inverlochy Castle, and the Campbells went down one after another under the sword thrusts of their hereditary foes, Sir Duncan dying bravely amidst his men.

Montrose granted quarter readily enough to the terrified Lowlanders, but there was no holding the exultant enemies of Clan Campbell. Montrose's army that bright Candlemas morning lost only four men, but fifteen hundred Campbells were slain in a bloody pursuit from the slopes of Ben Nevis to the shores of Loch Leven. Argyll's reputation in the Highlands was blasted, and the military power of Clan Campbell destroyed.

The same morning breeze that took the Marquess of Argyll in his lymphad shamefully down Loch Fyne also served to flutter out bravely the Red Lions of the Royal Standard when Montrose ran his banner up to the highest turret of Inverlochy Castle.

Argyll still had power in the Kirk, and the Kirk had power in the Lowlands. Montrose may have won the battle of

Inverlochy, but thanks to Argyll's intrigues, he was solemnly degraded from the nobility, his estates were confiscated, and some of his lands actually handed over to Argyll himself, 'to defray expenses'. The Marquess of Montrose, if taken alive, was to be hanged, drawn, and quartered – that is exactly what his enemies did to Montrose in the end, though only after years of hectic campaigning.

But that night in Inverlochy Castle all was triumph. As his Irish troops gathered to sing a Te Deum, Montrose sat alone, the Protestant among them, and wrote his dispatch to King Charles. The calm, grey-eyed aristocrat, as capable of writing a memorable poem as of fighting a battle against spectacular odds, was to be a legend in his lifetime. His chaplain, George Wishart, wrote in Latin an account of his campaign, which was read with delight all over Europe.

King Charles, a like-minded romantic, took these brilliant victories as a sign that his cause would triumph. Charles thereafter was continually making plans for sharing his fate with Montrose in the Highlands.

At Inverlochy, the wild clansmen had won a spectacular victory over the world of thrift and piety and law and trade. These were virtues that Argyll as a good Presbyterian was trying to implant among his clansmen, but they represented a style of life abhorrent to the Highlanders and the Irish, as indeed to the English Cavaliers.

But the battle for Scotland had to be won in the Lowlands, and there the Presbyterian Kirk, representing thrift and piety and law and trade, controlled the minds of men and influenced all their actions. Montrose was in the same predicament as the King he served – he was trying to save a vanishing world. Once Montrose brought his army of wild romantic Catholic Royalists down out of their Highland sanctuary, the rules of the game he played would be changed.

CHAPTER NINE

Armed Justice

Behold now this vast city, a city of refuge, the mansion
house of liberty ... the shop of war hath not there more
anvils and hammers working to fashion out the plates and
instruments of armed justice in defence of beleaguered truth
than there be pens and heads there, sitting by their studious
lamps, musing, searching, revolving new notions and
ideas ... – JOHN MILTON, *Areopagitica* (1644) describing
London during the Civil War

Christmas was slain at Naseby Fight – Popular saying (1646)

THE Reverend Hugh Peter was a Cornish Puritan who went
out to Massachusetts and took Roger Williams's place as
minister at Salem. In 1641 Hugh Peter went back to London
from Massachusetts on a diplomatic mission, but soon afterwards he decided to put on the plush coat and red montero
hat of a chaplain in the New Model Army. Eventually he
became Cromwell's closest adviser.

Several of the best officers in the Massachusetts volunteer
militia had followed Hugh Peter's example, bringing across
to England their experience in the Indian wars. When the
New Model Army was organized, most of these American
veterans joined the regiment of foot commanded by Thomas
Rainsborough.

Colonel Rainsborough had formerly been a sea-captain
and once had fought the Moorish pirates. He was radical
both in religion and politics, and his lieutenant-colonel was
Israel Stoughton, who back in Massachusetts had been
a magistrate. Rainsborough's major was another New

Englander, Nehemiah Bourne, a ship's carpenter by trade. The officers in Rainsborough's regiment were bold, practical, and ingenious men, and the regiment soon became expert at the risky business of assaults on fortified towns.

In England a man who owned a freehold property was exempt by law from the press-gang, but this meant that only one man in five in the countryside and one man in seven in a town was safe. All others could be dragged off by force and made to serve against their will in the ranks of the New Model Army. Pressed men served in the infantry. Cavalry troopers had to be men of some property, since they bought their own horse and buffcoat. Each cost about £10 – more than a skilled journeyman earned in a year.

After 7,000 reliable footsoldiers had been transferred from the disbanded forces of Essex and Waller, who both retired in April 1645, the New Model Army was still 14,000 men short. Of these, 8,460 were swept up by the press-gang. Thousands of young working men were carried off bodily from the streets of London. In Kent, where Royalist sentiment was strong, the pressed men mutinied.

Men who had been press-ganged into the army were not obliged to swear to the Covenant, and some managed to desert. But those who did put on the red uniform coat of the New Model Army and made the best of their new life found they were in quite a different world from the streets of London.

The tone in the barracks was set by those old soldiers – about one in a dozen – who were volunteers and had served in Parliament's army out of profound personal conviction. They were men who had settled on some kind of individual faith after private study of the Bible. They had not only fought battles but seen visions.

Some of these fervent old soldiers spoke of fighting for the New Jerusalem, or for the reign of King Jesus. Others had come back of their own accord from frontier America, where they had seen that a man could make a new life for himself here on earth with broad-axe, plough, and gun.

In the New Model Army, biblical quotations and loud extempore prayer and impassioned argument never ceased. The new army slowly came to resemble a kind of parallel Parliament, where earnest-minded Englishmen who understood the power of the sword looked at all the burning issues of the war in terms of Bible teaching, and where the young working men dragged by force off the streets of London listened and learned.

Regiments of the New Model Army that had formerly served under Waller or Essex were still officered by gentlemen. But some of the best regiments were not, and in England this was new. Okey and Pride, among the colonels, had been draymen; Hewson, a cobbler. Never before had craftsmen and tradesmen and yeomen risen to high command in an English army. Before the Civil War, only gentlemen carried swords.

Lieutenant-Colonel John Lilburne had resigned his command of the New Model's thousand-strong regiment of dragoons, and stocky, loud-voiced John Okey was promoted to take his place. No one who had seen John Lilburne's sublime courage at Brentford or Marston Moor supposed for one moment that he had lost his nerve and was now afraid to fight. Lilburne, in fact, had resigned in defence of a principle.

All officers were obliged to swear to the Covenant, the hypocritical oath that was the price of help from a Scots army. This John Lilburne stalwartly refused to do. He resented any such enforced oath as an encroachment upon his personal freedom. So Lilburne said good-bye to his dragoons and went to London to set up a clandestine printing press. From that time on, he was always in trouble with the authorities, but he became the conscience of the army – the eloquent spokesman for the rank and file.

One soldier in five was literate. But Lilburne's vivid and inflammatory pamphlets were read aloud by his old comrades in barracks and encampments, and soon the soldiers began to regard what Freeborn John had to say about liberty and property and government 'as gospel'.

In March of 1645, Prince Rupert was confronted by a strange and portentous uprising as he led his Cavaliers through Herefordshire. Fifteen thousand countrymen, small farmers, led by their parish clergy and armed with scythes and flails, had forced their way into the city of Hereford. They declared that they had gone to Hereford, their market town, so as to keep out the armies both of King and Parliament. They called themselves Clubmen. They had suffered for too long from plunderers both Roundhead and Cavalier, and now they simply wanted to be left alone.

By this time, the country folk up and down England had learned to detest the very sight of soldiers. Fighting men could legally be quartered on cottagers without payment, and soon ate up all their stocks of food. Horses urgently needed for ploughing were commandeered, flocks of sheep were slaughtered. If soldiers passed only one night at 'free quarters', a village could be pushed nearer the hunger-line.

The King's army had the worse name, especially in the west, where they were led by that champion plunderer, George Goring. Hardly ever paid, the King's men were now living off the country instead of fighting to save it. The mercenaries on both sides who learned their trade in the continental wars had long ago learned to take plunder for granted. They well knew how to extort a living from peasants with the sword.

But in an economic sense, many of the King's courtiers had been parasites before the war too. They lived off pensions and monopolies and gave little in return except by being decorative. In wartime, plunder appealed to their minds.

Sir Thomas Fairfax, now put in command of the New Model Army, made it his policy to win the country people over. He had always sympathized with the sufferings of poor folk. On his soldiers he imposed a strict discipline. Plunderers were henceforward to be shot. Seizing a farmer's horses or cutting down his fruit trees was to be punished as a serious crime.

Fairfax's men still had to live at 'free quarters' in villages, however, because Parliament was slack about sending down their pay. But many of the New Model soldiers were yeomen's sons, and they spoke in the same terms as the hard-done-by country folk. So the men of Fairfax's army became the first soldiers in the Civil War to win active sympathy in the countryside, and soon they began to think of themselves, not as mercenaries serving merely for pay and plunder, but as an army representative of the people.

After Marston Moor, the King had one army, based at Oxford, that was still unbeaten. Would Black Tom Fairfax succeed in bringing it to battle?

Parliament was timid about pitched battles and ordered Fairfax to start by besieging the King's headquarters at Oxford. The city was so short of food and so full of noblemen that a Royalist sentry, standing on the city wall to watch a Roundhead down below cook and eat his dinner, shouted across to him 'Fling me up half a mutton and I will fling thee down a lord.'

Since Fairfax had been given no heavy guns to batter down

the walls of Oxford, King Charles might have sat it out there for as long as his food lasted. But Charles impulsively decided to ride north, hoping to join forces with Montrose, who had won such glittering victories for him in Scotland.

On 9 May 1645, Charles and Rupert moved out of Oxford with most of the royal army. The court astrologer had predicted a disaster for London and a victory for the King, but Charles before he left had unwisely let himself be talked into giving George Goring the command of a separate army of cavalry in the west. Cavalry had been King Charles's strength, and now it was divided.

Prince Rupert never underestimated his enemy. He was much less cheerful than other Cavaliers about the outcome of doing battle with an army officered by psalm-singing draymen and prophesying cobblers. The more foolhardy Cavaliers believed that only gentlemen were fit to command soldiers and looked on the New Model Army as a bad joke. Some of them had recklessly been urging King Charles to risk a battle 'of all, for all' as the best way of winning back his kingdom.

Prince Rupert at last persuaded the King that he should order Goring to bring his troopers up from the west, so as to reinforce the royal army moving north. But George Goring, though a brilliant leader of horse, was a habitual drunkard, and when in his cups he was averse to orders that came even indirectly from Prince Rupert. So Goring lingered and loitered, and the lack of his cavalry weakened the royal cause.

On 30 May 1645, as the King's men marched through the Midlands, Prince Rupert managed by one emphatic act of aggression to put Parliament in a rage.

Leicester, inside its ring of medieval walls, appealed to Rupert much as Bolton had once done. Here was a stronghold of Puritanism, and therefore full of his enemies, but also a town long prospering from the wool trade, and so a juicy piece of plunder. His soldiers had not been paid, but they could at least be gratified with the plunder of Leicester.

After a three-hour cannonade, Rupert made a breach in the walls and at midnight the Prince led his men in. But the armed citizens of Leicester gave such stubborn resistance that Rupert's soldiers had to hack their way through the moonlit city towards the centre street by street. At last the Cavaliers rode their horses into the market place in triumph, but when the roll was called Rupert discovered that thirty royal officers had been killed.

The angry Cavaliers then took a terrifying revenge on the Puritans of Leicester. A hundred of them, including women and children, were cut down in the street. No girl was safe. Houses were emptied, shops stripped bare, and 140 carts filled with plunder from Leicester moved off to Newark Castle.

In Parliament there were important men who secretly might have no wish to see Tom Fairfax win another victory, but the sack of Leicester was too much. Shaken by the violence shown there by Rupert's Cavaliers, who by now regarded all Puritans with loathing and blamed them for the war, Parliament gave orders to Fairfax not to hang around Oxford any longer, but to take his army and go after King Charles.

Like Essex, Manchester, Waller, Haselrig, and indeed all other officers who were Members of Parliament as well, Oliver Cromwell had been obliged, by a new law, to lay down his commission. But in this emergency, the New Model had urgent need of him as a cavalry general. Fairfax's council of war signed a petition asking for Cromwell to command the horse, and Parliament consented.

This put Cromwell in an exceptionally strong political position – the basis for his future dictatorial power. He was now the key man, the army's only spokesman in Parliament, and Parliament's only representative in the army. He became a man courted by both sides, and carefully listened to, because he had armed power to back up his arguments.

The soldiers of the New Model, however, still regarded Oliver Cromwell as a man who thought and spoke like themselves – a straightforward and religious middle-aged officer who was also an invincible leader of cavalry. As Cromwell rode into camp at the beginning of June with 600 newly recruited East Anglian troopers, his old comrades 'gave a mighty shout at his coming.'

Major Leonard Watson, commanding the New Model's scouts, reported that Goring, though ordered to ride his 3,000 cavalry up from the west, had been on a four-day drunken debauch in Bath. Major Watson had intercepted a dispatch from Goring to King Charles, imploring him to postpone the clash between the two armies. If the King was short of cavalry, this was the moment to strike.

The Ironsides moved so fast that their vanguard surprised twenty Cavaliers playing quoits on a green outside a village inn, their tankards of ale on the table. They were an outlying royal cavalry picket, and so confident their nearest enemy was many miles away that they were not bothering to keep watch.

On paper, the royal army numbered about 11,000 to the New Model's 13,000, but many of the King's soldiers had sneaked off home with their rich plunder from Leicester. As usual, there were too many royal officers and not enough rank and file, and since Goring had not yet brought up his 3,000 horse, for once the King was weak in cavalry.

Roundhead and Cavalier met one another in battle array at last on a broad open field, north of the village of Naseby in the geographical centre of England. Streams on one side of the plateau flow down to the Bristol Channel; streams flowing down the other side eventually reach the North Sea.

Parliament's thirty-three-year-old general, Sir Thomas Fairfax, was riding a chestnut mare that day. He reined in on top of a gentle slope – the great field sloped down to a ditch and up the other side – to observe the confronting armies as they arranged themselves in battle-line.

Across the field ran a hedge – and Fairfax could see that Oliver Cromwell had already sent off John Okey and his dragoons at a fast gallop to seize it. Fairfax saw Okey's men dismount, one dragoon in ten holding the bridles of ten horses, while the other nine lined the hedge with their carbines. Cromwell, with his quick grasp of practical reality, had posted those dragoons so as to rake Prince Rupert's horsemen as they charged.

The mass of foot – pikemen and musketeers – in the Roundhead centre were led by old Philip Skippon, decent, staunch, and brave. But Skippon today had a much harder task than when he commanded his bold and well-trained apprentice lads at Newbury. Far too many of those Roundhead infantrymen were raw young soldiers, press-ganged, and still ignorant of their drill. Some of them had been given their weapons only when on the march to Naseby. The royal infantry facing Skippon was still under the command of old white-haired Jacob Astley, now Lord Astley, and his soldiers looked the better men.

Tom Fairfax astride his mare could see the regiments of Roundhead cavalry on his left forming into a line. Those were the troopers who would have to face the assault of Prince Rupert's Cavaliers. They had Okey's thousand dragoons in ambush behind that hedge to help them, but their commander, only just appointed, had not been proved in battle. He was a brave and logical, if sometimes unimaginative officer called Ireton – the man who was just about to marry Cromwell's plain and pious daughter Bridget. Ireton would do his best in this battle, but he was no genius.

All would therefore depend today on Oliver Cromwell's Ironsides, together on the right. Their chargers were stamping and shuffling impatiently, but the helmeted men themselves were as still as statues. The scope of Cromwell's charge would be impeded to the right by a rabbit warren, a bad obstacle, because a horse can stumble in a rabbit hole and throw its rider.

Cromwell's 3,500 Ironsides outnumbered the 1,500 Royalist cavalry they were facing – northcountrymen, under that grim-visaged veteran Sir Marmaduke Langdale. But because of the rabbit warren Cromwell would have to charge on such a narrow front that his numerical advantage was cancelled out.

Looking directly across the great field to the top of the facing slope, Tom Fairfax observed King Charles as he took his place for the battle. Conspicuous in gilt armour and astride a splendid Flemish charger, the King commanded the small Royalist reserve – men to be thrown into the fray when the contest wavered. Near where the King reined in fluttered a huge scarlet Royal Standard, flaunting its gold Lion and Crown.

Since the raw infantry massed in the centre of Parliament's army was beginning to look nervous at a mere distant view of the enemy, Sir Thomas Fairfax decided on a risky manoeuvre. His battle-line was formed and the Cavaliers were riding to take up their formation – but Fairfax ordered all his men to pull back a hundred paces.

This order was so unexpected and so unorthodox that a galloper came over hurriedly from old Sir Philip Skippon to question it. But Fairfax knew exactly what he was doing. The risk was worth taking. That hundred yards would make all the difference.

To the watching Cavaliers, the Roundhead army disappeared from sight over the crest of the far slope. The

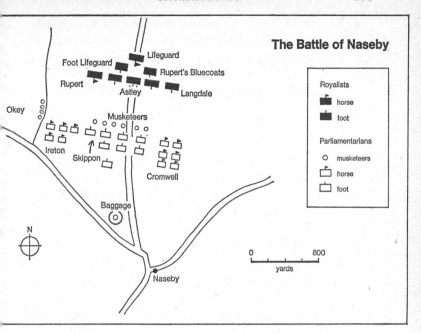

*The battle of Naseby, in the geographical heart of England,
where the decisive battle between King and Parliament was
fought*

nerves of the raw infantry in the centre were no longer shaken
by the novel sight of an enemy mustering for battle, and the
enemy could no longer see and judge Sir Thomas Fairfax's
dispositions. Fairfax announced as his field word 'God Our
Strength', and sent forward three hundred skirmishers, who
appeared, musket in hand, over the brow of the long slope,
the only Roundheads visible to the Cavaliers. King Charles,
ever mindful of his beloved wife, had given as his field word
'Queen Mary'.

Gigantic, dark-complexioned, his long ringlets flowing under the brim of his helmet, Prince Rupert that day was riding
a huge black horse as splendid and conspicuous as he himself

was. Rupert intended, as usual, to lead the charge in person. The Roundhead line withdrawing over the skyline might at one time have tempted Prince Rupert to make a premature attack, but since Marston Moor he had learned patience.

At ten o'clock, Fairfax's field guns managed to get off one round, but it was atrociously aimed and went zooming right over the heads of the Cavaliers. The three hundred Roundhead skirmishers were moving down the slope. The battle had begun. Prince Rupert raised his huge gloved arm as the signal – and the entire royal line moved forward as one man. Down their own side of the sloping field they went to the ditch at the bottom and up the far side, driving the skirmishers before them.

Prince Rupert, at the right of the line, had so far managed to keep his headstrong Cavaliers in hand, moving forward strictly in line with Lord Astley's infantry. Rupert looked up and saw the advancing Parliamentary battle-line, over a mile long, come impressively into sight over the crest of the facing slope. They too were on the move.

From somewhere to Rupert's right, as he led the royal line, came harassing carbine fire from Okey's men in hiding behind that hedge. Bullets whistled over the helmets of Rupert's Cavaliers as they trotted up the slope, and here and there in the line a horse stumbled, or a rider, struck by a lead slug, slumped uselessly down from the saddle.

The Cavaliers were beginning to go up the facing slope at a trot, when a loud command from Rupert brought them to a halt. 'Dress your line there! Dress your line!'

As if at drill, the Cavalier ranks paused, though under fire, to form straighter lines. Rupert meant their uphill charge to smite the enemy with the greatest possible simultaneous effect, and he was doing his best to impose on his Cavaliers some of the discipline shown by the Ironsides.

Ireton's horse, coming down to meet them, saw that the

Cavaliers had halted, and they paused irresolutely as if wondering what would happen next.

Rupert saw this and seized his chance. Rising in the stirrups to yell 'Charge!' he led his Cavaliers uphill at a trot that went in no time through a canter to a full gallop. One of Ireton's three regiments received that terrible charge at the halt 'and went clean away to Northampton and could never be stopped.' But the other two regiments began moving forward just in time, so that they collided with Rupert's men when at a trot and, though appallingly jarred by the impact, were able to fight back.

A glance over his shoulder told Prince Rupert that his own second line of cavalry was now coming up the hill behind him.

Ireton, not sensing danger from that second charge, but knowing the Roundhead centre to be weak, was trying to wheel his disorganized horsemen around to attack the flank of the royal infantry.

Ireton's attempt was a brave gesture, but misguided and foolhardy. Rupert's Cavaliers administered a second terrible clout to his shaken horsemen. Ireton's charger was shot from under him; he was run through the thigh with a pike, wounded in the face with a halberd, and taken prisoner. Cromwell's future son-in-law had managed to lose the cavalry battle on that side of Naseby field.

But Prince Rupert himself was unhappy. Could he merely have wheeled his own victorious horsemen to strike at and disperse the panicking Roundhead foot, this battle might have been won. But once launched at full gallop, Rupert's control over his headstrong Cavaliers was lost. Set them going in a charge and they were impossible to stop. Rupert saw his Cavaliers stream off the half-won battlefield towards the Roundhead baggage train, the thought uppermost in their minds at that moment being not victory but plunder.

Rupert galloped after and overtook his Cavaliers on his great black horse, hoping to scramble at least some of them back to the battlefield in time to play a worthwhile part. But in fact, Tom Fairfax, knowing well that this baggage train was a great temptation to the plundering Cavaliers, had set a trap. The baggage guards today were hand-picked men in tawny uniforms, armed with flintlocks, and they were posted there with orders to fight.

Yet for one breathless moment the trap failed to close. The baggage guard saw a cavalry general with black ringlets flowing from under his helmet come galloping urgently towards them and, taking him for Black Tom Fairfax, held their fire. But in the nick of time they recognized the rider as Prince Rupert, and gave him and his men a sharp welcome. By the time the Prince was able to extricate the more disciplined of his Cavaliers from the baggage train, form them up in troops, and lead them back on their blown horses to the battlefield, the King's cause was already in peril.

Sir Thomas Fairfax had lost his own helmet early in the day. His long black hair streaming in disorder, he rode his charger from one point of danger to another on the battlefield, giving exact and timely orders to the officers, laughing and joking with the soldiers, 'a spirit heightened above the ordinary spirit of men'.

Fairfax's own crack regiment of foot, to the right of the infantry line, were the only Roundhead pikemen still holding their ground. The King's Welshmen had pushed their way uphill and, by hacking and thrusting, broken Philip Skippon's line, the musketeers among them driving back the raw Roundhead levies with swinging blows of their musket butts. Skippon himself was wounded under the ribs by a musket bullet, which had pierced his armour. So as not to dishearten his men, Skippon managed to stay in the saddle and keep his place on the battlefield, but he was past giving orders.

The gusty north-west wind sent blinding clouds of gunpowder smoke into the Roundheads' faces, as infantry ensigns, flag in hand, moved back, trying hopelessly to rally their men to stand and fight. Reining in his chestnut mare, Fairfax peered apprehensively through the smoke towards the right wing of his army. Over there somewhere was Oliver Cromwell, and on Cromwell and his Ironsides alone the outcome of this battle now depended.

Two masses of horsemen in iron headpieces fired pistols point-blank into each other's armoured faces, then drew swords and started hacking away. The Ironsides and Sir Marmaduke Langdale's northcountrymen were at grips. But at a peremptory word of command from Oliver Cromwell, the buff-coated Ironsides broke off their hand-to-hand fight and coolly wheeled away to re-form ranks and charge anew.

Flesh and blood were not created to withstand the reiterated crash of those merciless short charges. Cromwell's troopers began pushing Langdale's obstinate northcountrymen backwards up their own slope. They were 'pressed hard before they got to the hill', declared an eyewitness laconically. 'They gave back.'

Under cover of Prince Rupert's Bluecoat Regiment, in the reserve, Sir Marmaduke Langdale tried hard to rally his troopers, but they had had enough. A final Ironside charge broke two of Langdale's squadrons, and the rest of the Royalist horse went streaming after the runaways in scared disorder.

The Ironsides then showed the remorseless puritanical discipline that won them battles. Cromwell ordered his front horsemen to chase Langdale's horsemen off the field. But that accomplished, they were to halt, re-form ranks, and come back promptly in fighting formation to join battle once more. This was a set of commands that in the heat of combat no Cavaliers could ever have taken seriously.

Cromwell was then able to use exactly the chance that Prince Rupert had seen but lost. Watching from across the battlefield, Sir Thomas Fairfax saw Cromwell turn and order the bulk of his horse, the second and third lines who were standing idly with loose bridles, jammed against that rabbit warren, to wheel and strike hard at the exposed flank of the royal infantry.

King Charles, too, commanding the reserve, could see clearly that the crisis of this battle had come. Somewhere over to the right, Rupert's Cavaliers had galloped away and not come back yet. Langdale was losing grip on the last of his own horsemen as they fled the field. The only royal cavalry still intact, a troop of Life Guards, was at that moment in the reserve under King Charles's personal command.

To charge with only one troop into the flank of Cromwell's Ironsides might be suicidal, but that was the only way to save the remnant of Langdale's horse. And with no Cavaliers in formation on the field, the battle and the Kingdom were lost.

'Face about!' shouted King Charles confidently to his Life Guards as Langdale's horsemen streamed past. 'Give me one charge more – and recover the day!'

Conspicuous in his gilt armour, Charles raised his drawn sword, and all the Life Guards at that moment were eager to follow their King. But the Scots Earl of Carnwath, at Charles's side, decided otherwise. Lord Carnwath 'on a sudden laid hand on his bridle, and swearing two or three full-mouthed Scottish oaths, said "Will ye go upon your death in an instant?"'

By tugging at the bridle, Lord Carnwath headed the King's Flemish charger away from the Ironsides, and all the Life Guards followed him in the wrong direction. King Charles's gallant and soldierly impulse was frustrated, and he lost the last chance that would ever be given him to die at the head of his men, a death he might well have preferred.

From his hedgerow on the far side of the field, Colonel John Okey could see that Cromwell's men had wheeled their steeds to charge the flank of the Royalist infantry. In his raucous Cockney voice he instantly ordered his thousand dragoons out of ambush.

Dragoons wore no armour and were never meant for charging across battlefields, but to his own delighted surprise, Sir Thomas Fairfax saw that Okey was leading his thousand men on their sorry nags in a reckless but inspired charge against the other exposed flank of the King's infantry.

By now Tom Fairfax had managed to rally some of Ireton's defeated cavalry. He led them, in company with his own crack regiment of foot, in a final tearing attack on all four sides of the fast-dwindling block of Royalist pikemen and musketeers. Cromwell's rear-rank Ironsides were charging the Royalist foot from one side, Okey's dragoons from another. Now came Tom Fairfax to join them, with more cavalry and the only intact regiment of Roundhead infantry. Fairfax headed this last charge himself. He fought exuberantly in the thick of it, putting an enemy ensign to the sword, and joyfully seizing his colour as a trophy. Prince Rupert's Bluecoats – the flower of the royal infantry, mostly Welshmen – withstood two such charges, but the third was too much.

Rupert, having succeeded in forming some of his runaway Cavaliers into troops, was leading them back from the baggage train to the battlefield. He could see at a glance that the day had clearly gone against King Charles. Rupert's men had frittered away an hour in the hope of plunder, and in that one hour all had been lost. For a mile across Naseby field, the royal foot were laying down their arms and surrendering by whole companies.

Rupert led his errant but undefeated Cavaliers up the far slope, to where his uncle King Charles had managed to rally the cavalry reserve, together with the few of Langdale's horse who still had fight in them. The King was preparing to make a final stand.

Prince Rupert could see the Ironsides turn their horses' heads about and, with uncanny self-command, form line. As the gunsmoke lifted they could be seen responding in an unnerving silence and with parade-ground precision to orders given by Fairfax himself in his clear and high-pitched voice. Cavalry, dragoons, and Roundhead foot – including Rainsborough's regiment, with its American contingent – were deliberately coming into formation, the cavalry on horseback waiting stock-still until the infantry had finished off their work of taking prisoners. There was still one last piece of work to do, and the battle of Naseby would be over.

Rupert, the King, and the bravest of the Cavaliers, knowing their turn would come next, meanwhile took up formation at the top of their slope and watched and waited.

The horsemen rallied around Rupert and Charles were the last remnant of the King's army. The Roundheads advanced uphill towards them in good order – cavalry, foot, and dragoons – as if it were still ten o'clock in the morning and the battle only just beginning. Strict silence was maintained until both sides were in range. Then one more raucous word of command came from John Okey, and his thousand dragoons fired a murderous carbine volley from the saddle.

All through the war from Edgehill until this moment, Rupert's famous Cavaliers had borne all before them. They were gentlemen serving their King on horseback. They were fearless. But as they watched Cromwell's Ironsides – cavalry of a new sort, where officers and troopers all looked alike –

come up the slope at them grimly and coldly, their stiff walk increasing to a controlled trot, the Cavaliers' nerve broke.

Prince Rupert, out in front, lifted his gauntleted hand and ordered them loudly and imperatively to charge. For the first time in the war, the Cavaliers refused. The King repeated the command and he was ignored. Most of the Cavaliers had not so far been defeated physically on Naseby field, but they were demoralized. Their will to fight had been broken.

The cavalry grouped around Rupert and Charles impulsively wheeled off to the right and streamed away. Prince Rupert accompanied the King and the Royal Standard away from Naseby. By one o'clock on the afternoon of 14 June 1645, the fight for the kingdom was over.

Oliver Cromwell then gave his cavalry orders to pursue – having first warned them that any trooper dismounting to plunder would be put to death. The chase was ruthless. The first eleven miles of the road to Leicester were littered with three hundred Cavalier dead, chopped down from behind as they ran. But three miles outside the plundered city, Lord Lichfield persuaded the Life Guards to turn and make a stand. The Ironsides, who had galloped their horses into a lather, were checked at last, and some of the Cavaliers escaped.

But five hundred of King Charles's officers, the veterans who by now understood war and could have created another army for him out of raw recruits, were made captive that day, and the King lost all his guns.

Though the Ironsides, in obedience to Cromwell's word, disdained to plunder, all the way across Naseby field the Roundhead foot were pillaging their 4,500 prisoners and stripping the corpses of the 1,000 Cavalier dead. They were, in fact, plundering the plunderers, since, as an eyewitness pointed out, 'No Royalist prisoner but had forty shillings on him, after Leicester.'

Many Court ladies and officers' wives were captured not far off, sitting in their coaches, waiting for a royal victory to be announced. They were made to buy their lives – and yielded up a pillage of £100,000 in gold, silver, and jewels.

A victory such as this was a visible proof to the Roundheads that God was on their side. Many believed literally that they were fighting God's enemies, as the Jews had done in the Old Testament. But Parliament's great victory at Naseby was stained by one act of heartless cruelty.

The Roundhead foot went off in a crowd to plunder the royal baggage park and found sheltering there a crowd of raggedly dressed women, whom they took for Irish Catholics because they spoke an unknown language, had 'cruel countenances', and tried to defend themselves with kitchen knives. They were almost certainly not Irishwomen, but the Welsh-speaking wives of poor Welsh conscripts. A hundred of these unlucky women were put to the sword. Officers' wives and some camp followers who had also taken shelter in the baggage park were, if not killed, deliberately gashed in the face, so as to be never again attractive to men. To these Puritan soldiers in their mystical bloodlust, any woman, whether lady or beggarmaid, who chose to follow a royal army could only represent Sin Incarnate.

From all over England came word that royal garrisons were yielding to Parliament. The Cavaliers had lost heart. Prince Rupert frankly advised the King his uncle to treat for peace, arguing sensibly 'I believe it a more prudent way to retain something than to lose all.'

The King's reply to his nephew was no less candid, and revealed Charles's deepest beliefs. 'Speaking either as a mere soldier or statesman, I must say there is no probability but of my ruin. Yet as a Christian, I must tell you, that God will not suffer rebels and traitors to prosper, nor this cause to be overthrown. And whatever personal punishment it shall please Him to inflict upon me must not make me repine, much less give over this quarrel.'

So long as Charles remained King of England, there was no hope of a negotiated peace based on concession and compromise. He would fight for what he believed until he died. His field army was lost, but Bristol, the second city in the kingdom, was still his. King Charles sent Rupert off to command the garrison.

Until now, King Charles had trusted Prince Rupert. But as the royal cause went wrong, ambitious or vicious men around the King were only too glad to spread mistrust. Their whispers against Prince Rupert began. They spread the story that his heart was no longer in the fight because he was expecting Parliament to crown his elder brother, the Elector Palatine, as a puppet king. This sounded all the more plausible since it was once what Sir Harry Vane had secretly planned.

Prince Rupert had informed King Charles that Bristol might be expected to hold out for four months, but Rupert found when he got there that Bristol's defences were by no means as strong as they looked on paper. He expected to find a garrison of 2,300 to man the five-mile-long wall, but most of his men were raw Welsh levies, and some deserted every day. Of the 800 poor Bristolians who had been pressed into service, many sympathized with Parliament. Rupert probably had only 1,500 reliable soldiers. And the plague had broken out.

The real difficulty was that country folk were no longer bringing in provisions to feed the city. The people were so sick of long years of Cavalier foraging and downright plundering that for miles around they had turned to welcome the New Model Army as deliverers. Not only were they helping Fairfax and his men with news and food, but two thousand westcountrymen were marching in with him as volunteers.

On 28 August 1645, Sir Thomas Fairfax took the fort at Portishead, thus closing Bristol off from the sea. Five Parliamentary warships blockaded the river mouth. At the head of an army of 12,000, Fairfax called on Prince Rupert to surrender the city.

Only a few days before, King Charles had marched back to Oxford, after trying and failing yet again to cut his way north and join Montrose. Prince Rupert politely offered to pass on Sir Thomas Fairfax's demand for surrender to the King, but Fairfax had no intention of letting Rupert play foxily for time. Fairfax gave orders to his army that when a signal beacon of straw and faggots was lit at 2 a.m. on the morning of 10 September Bristol was to be taken by assault.

The experts in this branch of warfare – a brigade of four regiments led in their work by Rainsborough and his Americans – began their attack by training four huge siege guns on the Cavaliers' strongpoint of Prior's Hill Fort. Their bombardment smashed the fort to smithereens. For two merciless hours, in a darkness lit only by the garishly flickering straw-and-faggot beacon, the Roundheads fought at push of pike along the wall before they managed to break inside the perimeter of the defences. Once the wall was broken through, the fighting was soon over.

Early on 11 September 1645, Oliver Cromwell and a group of his cavalry officers waited by the gate of Bristol Castle to receive the keys of the city. Out of the gateway in their red tunics clattered Rupert's escort of Life Guards. Then came Prince Rupert himself, a defeated giant of a man, 'clad in scarlet, very richly laid in silver lace, mounted on a very gallant black Barbary horse.'

So as to widen the rift between Rupert and the King, Parliament shrewdly chose the moment of his surrender to vote Rupert's brother, the Elector, a pension of £8,000. 'The House of Palatine', King Charles exclaimed in cold rage, 'seem to think themselves assured of the Crown.' From then on, Charles found himself unable to disbelieve the malicious whisperers. Word spread that Prince Rupert had sold Bristol to the enemy.

Prince Rupert had been given Sir Thomas Fairfax's permission to retreat with his men and all their baggage to Oxford. Black Tom Fairfax rode the first two miles of the way with the Prince, yielding him the place of honour on his own right, and talking to him amicably. When word of this courtesy reached King Charles, his suspicions deepened. Rupert told Fairfax that he was convinced the war would soon be over. He asked for the loan of some muskets to defend his marching men against Clubmen as they went through open country. He promised to give them back at Oxford – and the promise was kept.

King Charles, now at Newark Castle, sent a curt and angry written order to Prince Rupert, telling him 'to seek your subsistence somewhere beyond the seas, to which end I send you herewith a pass.' This affront to his honour was too much for Prince Rupert. With a handful of friends he cut his way recklessly through enemy-held territory to meet his uncle face to face at Newark and show him clear proof that at Bristol there had been no treachery whatever.

But the days of unhesitating trust were over. Rupert at the end of the war had not fifty pounds in his pocket. He had fought with a mind above mercenary advantage. Soon after, he gave up the fight and went abroad.

In October 1645 Oliver Cromwell brought up the army's heavy siege guns to attack Basing House, the mansion of an old Roman Catholic peer, the Marquess of Winchester, and one of the last fortified places in all England still holding out

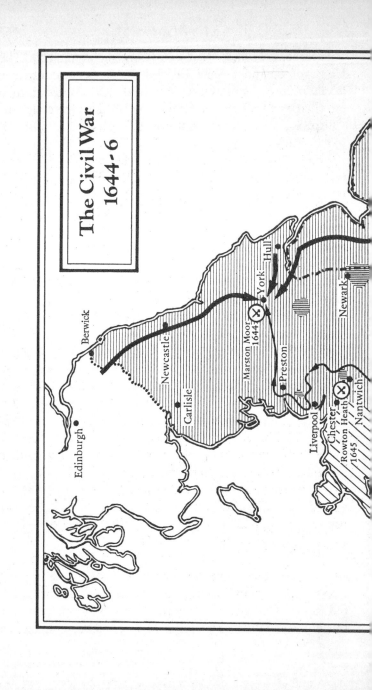

The Civil War
1644-6

Edinburgh

Berwick

Newcastle

Carlisle

Marston Moor
1644

York

Hull

Preston

Liverpool

Chester

Rowton Heath
1645

Nantwich

Newark

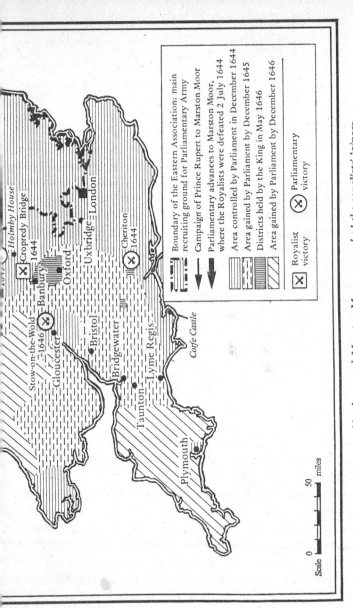

Legend:

Boundary of the Eastern Association: main recruiting ground for Parliamentary Army

Campaign of Prince Rupert to Marston Moor

Parliamentary advances to Marston Moor, where the Royalists were defeated 2 July 1644

Area controlled by Parliament in December 1644

Area gained by Parliament by December 1645

Districts held by the King in May 1646

Area gained by Parliament by December 1646

☒ Royalist victory   ⊗ Parliamentary victory

Map locations: Holmby House, Cropredy Bridge 1644, Banbury, Oxford, Uxbridge, London, Stow-on-the-Wold 1646, Gloucester, Bristol, Bridgewater, Taunton, Lyme Regis, Cheriton 1644, Corfe Castle, Plymouth

Scale 0 — 50 miles

Two Parliamentary victories – at Newbury and Marston Moor – wrecked the royalists' 'pincer strategy'. From their strongholds in London and East Anglia the Roundheads gradually pushed the Cavaliers back towards Wales and the West of England.

for King Charles. London merchants particularly resented the Cavaliers who occupied Basing House, because throughout the war their raids had hampered London's profitable wool trade with the west.

By 13 October, after a seven-day bombardment, Cromwell's men succeeded in making two breaches in the walls of the old mansion. Before leading his men in a dawn assault, Cromwell spent the whole night in prayer and meditation. To his tense and puritanical mind came images of Basing House as a place full of idols and idolators. He pictured the mansion to himself, in a visionary way, as a 'nest of Romanists' that it was his bounden duty to destroy utterly.

Orders were given that everyone inside the walls of Basing House, man or woman, was to be treated as an enemy. The dawn attack was violent, and the rule was: Give no quarter. A clergyman's daughter gave a defiantly insolent answer to Colonel Harrison, a butcher's son from Staffordshire, and the Colonel ran her through with his sword. He went on afterwards to cut down Robbins, the once popular London actor, who had found refuge in charitable Basing House when the Puritans closed the theatres.

Six of the ten Roman Catholic priests who had found sanctuary in the mansion and celebrated mass in its chapel – a capital crime – were killed that morning in cold blood. The other four were made prisoner, to be publicly hanged, drawn, and quartered later on in front of an eagerly appreciative London mob.

When a hundred of the occupants had been killed outright and three hundred made prisoner, Basing House was rapidly and efficiently turned into cash. The garrison's rations of bread and cheese were sold off to countrymen living nearby. The furniture, tapestries, and bedding were auctioned to dealers who came swarming down from London. Women prisoners were stripped to the skin for the sake of their fine clothes – as was the aged Marquess of Winchester himself. A hundred women's dresses were in this way accounted for among the variegated plunder sold to dealers, who even gave a price for the lead on the roof and the iron bars in the windows. The sale went on for days.

Plucked of the fine clothes, which all his life had marked him in others' eyes as a gentleman, the Marquess of Winchester looked no better than any other pathetic naked old man, but he still kept his high aristocratic spirit. Hugh Peter, the minister from Salem, now Cromwell's chaplain, picked on this moment of his enemy's downfall to ask the Marquess candidly if he did not now think his cause must be hopeless.

'If the King had no more ground in England but Basing House,' was the old man's dignified reply, 'I would adventure it as I did, and so maintain it to the uttermost.' Prophetically he told Hugh Peter that 'the King would have his day again.'

One other sick and naked old man was carried out of Basing House in a blanket. He was Inigo Jones, the architect who had designed Covent Garden, and who once, in King Charles's heyday, had drawn up for him a set of plans, never to be realized, for making London a capital city as beautiful architecturally as Paris.

Special attention was given by the Ironsides to those paintings in the Marquess of Winchester's collection, mostly Italian masterpieces, that depicted religious themes, for instance of the Virgin Mary and the Infant Jesus, which for doctrinal reasons were offensive to the Puritans. These were all sent off in a wagon to London, along with a heap of missals and rosaries, to feed a public bonfire. When nothing was left of Basing House that would fetch a fair price or set a pious example, the ruined shell was set on fire.

The society that England had inherited from so many past centuries – her old Catholic culture of status and deference, saints' days and Christmas pudding, cathedrals, craft guilds, and agricultural backwardness – was gone for ever from Basing House, as indeed from all over the land. Something new had arrived.

Puritans, despisers of the pleasures of the eye and of the flesh, men who lived by Bible and ledger, had at last gained in great measure the freedom for which in their own view of the matter they had gone to war.

This was not freedom as John Lilburne and the common people who read his pamphlets understood the word. Men of importance on the winning side wanted greater freedom to trade, to improve, and to exploit, untrammelled by traditional moral or social restraints. And once the war was over, that was what they could hope to enjoy.

Merrie England was at its last gasp; the modern world was screaming and kicking in its cradle.

Worcester had been the first town in England to declare for King Charles. Defended furiously by Colonel Henry Washington, it was the last town to yield. On 24 March 1646, the very last handful of royal troops at large was rounded up at Stow-on-the-Wold.

Their officer was another Roman Catholic, sixty-seven-year-old Jacob Astley, who had fought valiantly for his King since swords were first drawn at Edgehill. The white-haired veteran sat himself down on a drumhead amid his Roundhead captors, and said to them gently, as if to his own grandchildren, 'You have done your work, boys, and may go play – unless you will fall out among yourselves.' It was a shrewd prediction.

In 1645 Montrose came down into the Lowlands and took the city of Glasgow – his last big success. He then moved with not quite enough men towards the Border, to keep his

promised rendezvous with King Charles. Alasdair Mac-
Donald had taken all the Highlanders and many of the Irish
to make a raid into Galloway.

Montrose entered England on 5 September 1645, at the
low ebb of the royal cause, with only 500 of his Irish infantry.
He had managed so far to recruit 1,200 not very enthusiastic
cavalry, mostly the sons of Royalist gentlemen. But the Lowland lairds had failed to persuade their tenantry to arm and
ride out for King Charles. The poor countrymen would
rather listen to the voice of the Presbyterian Kirk. In his
whirlwind Scottish campaign Montrose had won battles and
taken cities, but he had failed to capture men's minds.

David Leslie, the Covenanting general who had helped
Cromwell so cleverly at Marston Moor, was out along the
Border hunting Montrose down with 5,000 cavalry and 1,000
foot. A Scots peer called Traquair, who hitherto had pretended to have Royalist sympathies, decided to betray Montrose. Word came secretly to David Leslie, telling him exactly
where and how Montrose could be taken by surprise.

On the night of 13 September 1645, the five hundred Irish
had pitched their camp at Philiphaugh, a long water-meadow
where the River Ettrick meets the River Yarrow. Montrose
and his volunteer cavalry had billets in the little town of Selkirk, on the hill above. At daybreak, out of a heavy mist,
Leslie's mass of cavalry broke upon the encamped Irish,
who were outnumbered by not less than eight to one.

Montrose called for his cavalry to follow him in a charge.
Down he came headlong from Selkirk to the mist-obscured
meadow of Philiphaugh, but the lairds' sons dragged their
feet. Only a hundred troopers – one man in a dozen – followed Montrose in his wild and desperate rescue.

The onset of those hundred horsemen actually drove back
the foremost Covenanting cavalry, and gave the Irish breath-

ing space. But numbers told. Each one of Montrose's swordsmen, on foot or on horseback, was blindingly outnumbered,
and most of them fought their last fight on that misty
meadow.

Over four hundred Irish had been killed, and only half of
Montrose's hundred troopers were left alive when the friends
grouped themselves protectively around Montrose and compelled him to turn off and cut his way out. With this handful
of comrades Montrose made for the safety of the hills. When
only fifty of Montrose's Irishmen were still left alive, David
Leslie called on them to surrender, offering them quarter.

To the Covenanting ministers who travelled with the army
a live Irish papist was an infamous affront. These ministers
had David Leslie's ear, and that day and the next they remon-
strated with all their eloquence against the quarter he had
allowed the survivors among Montrose's infantry. They hit
at last on a subtle argument. They persuaded Leslie that the
quarter he had granted applied only to the officer who actually had asked for it – to him personally, and to no one else.
So the Irish rank and file, according to this argument, had
not been granted quarter.

Weakly, David Leslie gave way, and next day his soldierly
good name was tainted throughout all history by a cold-
blooded massacre, when the last handful of Montrose's gallant Irish were shot down or hacked to pieces as they stood
unarmed in a castle courtyard.

Both their officers were later hanged as common criminals
in Edinburgh, though one of them at least, even by the Covenanters' own argument, must have been granted quarter.

Then at Linlithgow came the worst part. Three hundred
Irishwomen and their children, together with the Aberdeen
lasses who long since had chosen to follow Montrose, were
forcibly seized by Covenanting soldiers and thrown over the
bridge into the river. Those who knew how to swim were

pushed under with stabs from the soldiers' long pikes. In Scotland, too, the King's cause was lost, gone down in a welter of treachery and blood.

Montrose came back to fight another day, but his fellow-Presbyterians got him at last and dealt with him as they had always said they would. James Graham, who had been Marquess of Montrose until they degraded him from the nobility, was hanged, drawn, and quartered. Pieces of his severed body were stuck up over the gates of Edinburgh as a visible warning to all that the Kirk, not the King, ruled in Scotland.

CHAPTER TEN

Now for King Charles

I am not without hope that I shall be able so to draw the
Presbyterians or the Independents to side with me for
extirpating one another that I shall really be King again
— KING CHARLES to Lord Digby (March 1646)

... religion is the only firm foothold of all power; that cast
loose or depraved, no government can be stable; for when
was there ever obedience where religion did not teach it?
— KING CHARLES to Queen Henrietta Maria

IN the afternoon of 27 April 1646, a Cavalier called Jack
Ashburnham, a groom of the royal bedchamber, rode out of
Oxford and crossed Magdalen Bridge as the clock struck
three. On a nag behind him jogged a middle-aged servant
with cropped hair and a curious-looking beard, carrying
three valises.

The Governor of Oxford, Sir Thomas Glemham, came
down in person to lock the city gates behind them. He
shouted 'Good-bye, Harry!' to the second of the travellers.
The servant smiled. His name was not Harry but Charles,
and the beard was false. But the pass Jack Ashburnham carried was genuine enough. It was signed by Fairfax and gave
him permission as a Cavalier to ride to London and 'make his
composition' with the Parliamentary authorities – buy himself out of the war.

As they rode along, Jack Ashburnham tried to persuade
King Charles that his best chance lay in heading towards a
North Sea port like Lynn, where sympathizers would put him
on a boat to join the irrepressible Montrose, who, once again,

after his narrow escape at Philiphaugh, was making war on the King's enemies from a base in the Highlands.

Then, through the French Ambassador, the King received a tricky verbal assurance from Lord Leven's Covenanting army in the north of England. He would be received by Leven's Scots 'in safety and honour', and with no wrong done to his conscience. The Stuarts had been Kings in Scotland long before they reigned in England. With England lost, Scotland might become a refuge. Charles turned his horse's head north and, after riding hard all night, gave himself up to his fellow-countrymen at the Saracen's Head, in South-well. He was soon to regret it.

The Scots nobles had enriched themselves with church lands at the Reformation, so they had a strong motive ever after for supporting the Kirk, even though at times it might involve associating with the lower orders. Because Charles was an Episcopalian, they were deeply unsure of him. Might not a man so devoted to another system of religion one day demand back the lands in Scotland that belonged by historic right to the church?

The men of importance in Scotland therefore needed a Presbyterian King, who would guarantee their estates, put down dangerous social and religious opinions, like those that were spreading in the New Model Army, and do his best to see that Scotland was never swallowed up by England, her richer and more powerful neighbour.

Once they had Charles prisoner, the Covenanters' plan was first to get rid of his loyal servants, like Ashburnham, and then to break the King's will – force him, somehow, to turn his back on Montrose, sign the Covenant, and declare for a Presbyterian system in both his kingdoms.

The King's religious opinions were the chief obstacle to this plan, so they began by doing all they could to weaken the tenets of Charles's faith. Alexander Henderson, an eloquent Presbyterian divine, was famous all over Scotland as the preacher who years before had converted the Marquess of Argyll. Alexander Henderson now spent seven weeks with King Charles in unending disputation. He was helped by four other ministers in relays. The five of them preached at King Charles and argued with him and prayed aloud at him, never giving him a moment's peace.

All they needed was the result of one moment of weakness, a signature. If a man as conscientious as Charles signed the Covenant, that would bind him.

'I never knew,' Charles wrote secretly to his Queen, 'what it was to be barbarously treated before.'

Yet Alexander Henderson, for all his merciless urgency, failed to shake the King's belief. In fact, King Charles's burning sincerity and clarity of conviction began to shake Henderson. The famous minister had collided with a faith as intense and well thought out as his own, even if more modest in its expression. Henderson went back to Edinburgh baffled, and died there soon after 'of a broken heart'.

The Marquess of Argyll was controlling all this maltreatment of the King. Argyll now put forward an extremely clever argument. Evidently King Charles could not be shaken in mind. Might he be shattered in body? That verbal promise they had all made, to keep their King 'in safety and honour', would in the most literal sense be fully kept, he contended, even if Charles were thrown into prison, provided, of course, the King's attendants served him on bended knee ('honour') and carefully guarded him against assassination ('safety')!

Argyll, who had private dungeons of his own in the Highlands, was a great believer in the efficacy of prison. A rigorous prison, he believed, might break King Charles where prayers had failed. But for other Scottish lords, this proposal was too much.

Charles found Argyll 'very civil and cunning'. To his

Queen he wrote 'There never was a man so alone as I. All the comfort I have is in thy love, and a clear conscience.' Yet even resolute Queen Henrietta Maria was being pushed by her worldly advisers into recommending that the King get the worst over by signing the Covenant. Thousands of his subjects had already put their name to it, tongue in cheek. However, on a matter of principle – anything affecting his private beliefs – the King would never give an inch.

Charles's magnificent obstinacy saved him. In the English Parliament, Presbyterians and Independents alike wanted by now to get rid of the Scots army, which had hardly done its fair share of the fighting, yet was claiming over a million pounds as arrears of pay. This debt to Scotland was eventually settled at £400,000 and part of the agreement was that King Charles, now useless to the Scots, should be handed by them bodily to his English enemies as soon as the first £100,000 had been paid.

The King spent his last few days among his fellow-countrymen in comparative freedom, playing golf and twitting them for selling him too cheap. Lands confiscated from the Anglican bishops were sold off by Parliament to raise the cash for buying back the King. As the Scots army took their money and marched north out of Newcastle, the fishwives lined the streets and pelted the departing soldiers with stones, to loud cries of 'Judas!'

The soldiers of the New Model Army did no fighting whatever from midsummer 1646 to May Day 1648, but a great deal of arguing – and the tone of their arguments frightened the rich.

In 1646, the harvest failed completely, the first of six deplorable harvests in a row, and the plague reached London. The price of bread doubled. A sympathy of opinion and interest grew up in these hard times between London craftsmen, small shopkeepers, wage-earners, and the radicals in the army. They were all beginning to read pamphlets by John Lilburne and others like him and to discuss with a new earnestness what should be done about the state of the king-dom.

In England, before 1646, the common people did their best to earn a living and to bring up their families, and they left politics and government to their betters. But now, after their war experiences, the novel idea that they might have democratic rights, the right to a say in government, had be-gun to germinate among soldiers and citizens alike.

By the spring of 1647 the men of the New Model Army had grievances. The footsoldiers were owed eighteen weeks' arrears of pay, and the troopers forty-three weeks'. Once they got home, cavalry troopers who had laid out their own money for costly equipment would be in dire need of this back pay to set themselves up again in their workshops or on their farms.

Until now, soldiers who had lost arms or legs in battle and who owned no property had been put off with a 'licence to beg'. The men of the New Model Army were no longer prepared to have their unluckier comrades treated like this. And they wanted help for orphans and widows.

The New Model Army set up a council of senior officers, but also including two junior officers and two rankers, from each regiment. They were called Agitators, and since their strength lay in keeping the Army together, officers and men alike made a solemn agreement not to separate. The Pres-byterians in Parliament decided at once that they had better get rid of these discontented fighting men by sending them overseas, but when they called for volunteers to fight against the papist Irish, they found that only 167 officers out of 2,320, and hardly any rankers at all, were willing to go.

Many Puritans both in Parliament and the City had grown

rich from victory. For six months after the battle of Naseby, a Cavalier was allowed to make his peace by paying a heavy fine, varying from two years' rental of his estate to half its selling price, depending on his rank and importance. To pay this fine, Cavaliers had to borrow at heavy interest from City money-lenders or even to sell off part of their land so as to save the rest. Church and Crown lands were also briskly changing hands in the market. So the monied men on Parliament's side – lawyers, merchants, money-lenders and war-contractors – had been able to buy up manors cheaply, and could aspire to become landed gentry. Now, if only the rebels in Ireland could be crushed, there were millions of acres there too, waiting to be seized.

Oliver Cromwell had taken up the sword as an impoverished Puritan gentleman who sat in Parliament but hardly ever spoke, and earned his £300 a year by farming. But after Naseby an official gift was made him of £2,500 a year in land, taken from the confiscated estates of the old Marquess who had been captured and stripped naked at Basing House. This income brought Cromwell into the charmed circle of those who were doing well out of the war. Other army leaders who had gone up in the world like this were nicknamed 'grandees' by the rank and file. Some of Cromwell's shrewder Ironsides began to wonder how long their famous general would stay loyal to them.

Denzil Holles, who spoke for the rich Presbyterians in Parliament, said of the New Model Army that 'the meanest of men, the basest and vilest of the nation, the lowest of the people have got the power into their hands.' Holles believed that the Independents were out to 'ruin the King and as many of the nobility and gentry as they could, alter the Government, have no order in the Church nor power in the State over them.' He thought that any petition from the ranks of the army was a mutiny, to be punished by death. As for pay-

ing them their arrears, let them wait. This contempt for the
wishes and needs of the ordinary soldier was in the end to
cost Parliament dear.

The Army and Parliament were now the two powers in the
land. The tone of the Army was Independent, and the dominant party in Parliament (though there were also some
Independents in Parliament) was Presbyterian. King Charles
was a prisoner, but by clever manoeuvring he did his best to
play these two powers off against each other as if he were
still the most important piece on the board.

There can be no game of chess without the King. Charles
well knew that without a monarch at the head of the social
pyramid, men of property would never feel secure in their
possessions. He was also confident that the common people
still regarded him as their friend.

Holmby House, where the King had been sent under guard
as Parliament's prisoner, was an Elizabethan 'prodigy house',
an extravagant mansion built for Queen Bess by Sir Christopher Hatton. Charles was well guarded there, but not badly
treated. In the afternoon of 2 June 1646, the King was playing bowls on the lawn. His face was now haggard, and his
dark hair had begun growing out in silver streaks, but he was
in good spirits.

Watching his game of bowls were about fifty red-coated
dragoons. These men guarding the King were commanded
by a colonel called Graves, who had been given the job by
Parliament because he was a reliable Presbyterian.

Hoofbeats in the distance made dragoons and players all
turn and stare. Fifty yards away a party of New Model Army
troopers reined in, watched the game for a while, as if to
make sure that one of the men playing bowls was indeed
King Charles, and rode off.

These Ironsides were led by a young cornet of Fairfax's Life Guard called George Joyce, who in civil life had been a tailor. Cornet Joyce had already surrounded Holmby House with five hundred troopers hand-picked from different cavalry regiments in the New Model Army. He had come here to seize King Charles.

Rumours had come to Cromwell's ears in London that the Presbyterians were plotting to call the Scots army back and in some way wring an agreement out of King Charles by force. Once the Presbyterians in Parliament had a submissive King and a foreign army that would do their will, another civil war, between Independents and Presbyterians, was likely to break out. Cromwell declared to his friends 'We must break the back of this design', but he kept out of sight and let hotheaded young men in the New Model Army like Cornet Joyce do his work.

Ironsides came to Holmby House that night in secret to meet the guard of dragoons and talk them into joining their side. Since the fifty dragoons were men who had fought under Colonel Lilburne and Colonel Okey, they were easy to persuade. Early next morning the five hundred Ironsides closed in. Colonel Graves shouted urgent orders to his dragoons, but his orders were ignored, and he ran for his life.

George Joyce went into King Charles's bedroom to wake him and, speaking to him (he reported later) 'with as much gentleness and tenderness as he could', explained to the King that the men he commanded 'did desire to secure him from being taken away, lest he should be set at the head of another army.'

Next morning the five hundred young Ironsides representing the entire New Model Army were drawn up in good order outside Holmby House. Cornet Joyce asked them solemnly in the King's presence if they accepted King Charles's three conditions: that his person be not harmed nor his conscience forced, and that his servants go with him. They all shouted 'Yes!' and the King was happy to believe them.

Those young Ironsides, after all, had seen and admired the King's personal courage in battle, and Charles this morning seemed particularly glad of their company, telling the troopers cheerfully as he took his place among them on horseback that he could ride 'as far as you or any man.'

But behind his affable smile the King was already thinking how he might charm and use these young cavalrymen in his plots to set the Army against Parliament. Charles had this much in common with the Presbyterians; he too thought that his interests could best be served by getting the Civil War going again. But nothing was more certain to lose him the hearts of the ordinary people, who by now were getting desperate for peace.

When the Presbyterians in Parliament heard that young men from the Army had taken bodily possession of the King, they quickly offered the soldiers all their arrears of pay and threatened Oliver Cromwell himself with impeachment.

Taking Hugh Peter with him, Cromwell rode off at breakneck speed to Newmarket Heath, where the regiments in the New Model Army had come together to a rendezvous. Cromwell from then on came out publicly as the spokesman for his soldiers.

Of King Charles's six children, the pretty baby, Henrietta, had already been smuggled out to her mother in France. His eldest daughter Mary, who was married to William II, Prince of Orange, was living in Holland. The Prince of Wales was by now sixteen, and he, too, had got away. But his younger brother, James, Duke of York, had been less lucky, and along with the two small children, Elizabeth and Henry, he was now kept in London by Parliament as a hostage. The Army treated Charles with decent humanity, and gave him a chance to see his children. Eventually they offered him his throne again, and on better terms than he could expect to make with Parliament.

These radical young soldiers, easy-going about other men's religious beliefs so long as their own were tolerated too, would even go so far as to let Charles have his bishops back. But Charles then began to bicker about details. When he said 'You cannot do without me. You will fall to ruin if I do not sustain you', the soldiers began to see through his game. Because King Charles thought himself indispensable, he was only humouring them.

Charles had been expecting the men of the New Model Army to ask him for titles and honours. Their religious faith was as sincere as his own, but the minds of many of these soldiers were filling with newfangled democratic ideas that were incomprehensible to the King. He was baffled by their motives. He was living in the past.

King Charles himself had given the nickname of 'Levellers' to the radicals in London and the Army who followed John Lilburne. The name of Levellers had first been applied in years gone by to rebellious villagers who had gone out in armed gangs to level the lord of the manor's hedges and enclosures whenever he tried to filch their common lands. According to the Royalist newspaper who reported him, King Charles had explained that the Levellers 'would make us all even, so that every Jack shall vie with a gentleman, and every gentleman be made a Jack.'

John Lilburne's Levellers, England's first democratic political party, were organized at meetings in London taverns, and had begun to send out their pamphlets and petitions by stage coach all over England. The Levellers agreed heartily with the rank and file of the Army in wanting religious tolerance. But Lilburne's Levellers were the first party in the

Civil War standing not for one set of religious principles against another, but for freedom. Whereas others spread their views through the pulpit, the Levellers relied on the printing press.

Their spokesman in the House of Commons, Henry Marten, was a republican of no very decided religious views. But Marten tried on principle to secure fair treatment both for Roman Catholics, who risked prison or death if they celebrated mass, and for Jews, who then had no legal right even to enter England. Jews trading in London had long been obliged to worship in a secret synagogue.

Most men in Parliament thought poverty was a mark of God's displeasure; therefore, it was a crime not to pay one's debts. But Marten also spoke up bravely for the ten thousand unlucky Englishmen, often craftsmen or farmers ruined by the war, who had been put in prison for debt that had usually been no fault of their own. Once in prison they could neither support their families nor earn money to pay off the debt, so they could never become free again.

The Presbyterians were fast losing support in the country, but they still had a majority in Parliament. They thought of a clever way to crush their political opponents through a Parliamentary enactment that would penalize their religious opinions. They put forward a Blasphemy Ordinance, drafted in such terms that it automatically sent Unitarians to death and condemned Baptists to life imprisonment. For saying no more than 'that man by nature hath free will to turn to God' a man under this ordinance could go to prison for life.

The time was long past in England when religious principles could be forced on people by threats. At first the Presbyterians could not get enough votes to pass this barbarous ordinance, and when they did, it simply could not be enforced. But a persecuting Parliament loses its moral authority. The effect of the Blasphemy Ordinance was only to turn young Baptist and Unitarian and Congregational soldiers in the New Model Army against the control of Parliament and against the rule of law.

During July of 1647, the New Model Army began to march from Newmarket to London, declaring 'We are not a mere mercenary army, hired to serve any arbitrary power of a state, but the defence of our own and the people's just rights and liberties.' The burning question for the soldiers was no longer their back pay, but how best to govern the kingdom.

On 29 July, the group of Independents in Parliament, including Speaker Lenthall, eight peers, and fifty-seven Members of Parliament, fled from London to join the Army, now at Bedford, only fifty miles away, and coming closer. The Presbyterians were isolated.

When the Presbyterian Lord Mayor called out his trained bands, hoping to keep the New Model Army out of London as King Charles's Cavaliers had been kept out years before, only about one man in a dozen turned up on parade. The rank and file had been listening to the Levellers.

As the unenthusiastic trained bands, with nearly more officers than men, were parading in St James's Fields, waiting to be inspected by Massey and Waller, the vanguard of the New Model Army reached the outskirts of London. They were headed by Rainsborough's regiment of foot, a crack force commanded by a Leveller, officered by Americans, and expert at capturing cities.

The vanguard swung round to the south bank of the Thames. The London suburb of Southwark across the river was a Leveller stronghold. Friends inside Southwark opened the gate, and as Colonel Rainsborough and his men marched in, they were given a huge shout of welcome.

From a vantage point on the south bank of the Thames,

Rainsborough and his men mounted a battery of guns aimed at the defences of London Bridge. The sight across the river of those guns manned by determined young men in red coats was enough. All resistance in the City collapsed.

Eighteen thousand men of the New Model Army were soon marching in triumph through London with laurel leaves in their hatbands. The respectable poor were cheering, and the rich had sour faces. The Ironsides stabled their horses in St Paul's.

The Army withdrew from London not long after, leaving a regiment behind camped in Hyde Park, not far from Parliament, as a visible reminder of the Army's point of view. King Charles was brought nearer London, to his palace at Hampton Court.

But what was the Army's point of view?

Between 28 October and 11 November 1647, the Army Council, officers and men alike wearing high-crowned hats, sat round a table in cold and foggy Putney Church and debated this matter. A conflict of opinion emerged, reflecting a split in the Army, as everywhere else in England, between the haves and have-nots.

The argument centred around a constitutional plan that the soldiers had drawn up, called 'The Agreement of the People', to be urged on Parliament as the Army's view of how England should rightly be governed. The 'Agreement' now sounds not at all original, but in England, as in most other countries, the notions it expressed were then almost unheard of. The 'Agreement' was the first draft of a constitution for England that would be in some respects not unlike the American Constitution. The Army wanted a Parliamentary democracy.

This new Parliament was to be elected every two years from constituencies equal in size. Parliament would take over from the King his control of the armed forces, but grant freedom of conscience. An Act of Oblivion was to cancel out offences against the law of the land committed during the war by Roundhead and Cavalier alike, so that all Englishmen could be reconciled. Men should be equal before the law, and the press-gang was to be abolished.

Hitherto in England only freeholders, the minority of men owning house property or land, had been allowed to vote, and even freeholders were not always lucky. Cromwell's troopers, the Ironsides, were usually men of small property, so a good many of them had votes already. But most New Model soldiers in the infantry owned nothing but their weapons. The most articulate men among the rank and file, cavalry and infantry alike, wanted every Englishman to have the right to vote, and some of their officers agreed. On this issue, the Army Council split.

Cromwell's son-in-law, General Ireton, his face scarred from his wound at Naseby, was for giving votes only to 'the persons in whom all land lies, and those in corporations in whom all trading lies.' With cold but penetrating logic, he argued 'If you admit any man that hath a breath and being, this will destroy all property. Why may not these men vote against all property?'

Colonel Rainsborough the Leveller put the opposite point of view. 'Every man that is to live under a government,' he argued, 'ought first by his own consent to put himself under that government.' His younger brother, Major William Rainsborough, posed the question even more sharply. 'I would fain know what the soldier hath fought for all this while? He hath fought to enslave himself, to give power to men of riches, men of estates . . .'

Private Sexby, an Agitator, a man from the ranks, was no less forthright. 'There are many thousands of us soldiers that have ventured our lives. But it seems now, except a man hath a fixed estate in this kingdom he hath no right in this kingdom. I wonder we were so much deceived.'

Oliver Cromwell was willing to agree with the Levellers present that 'the foundation and supremacy is in the people, radically in them'. But he told them that the vote for every man 'did tend very much to anarchy.' Snug in the £2,500-a-year estate granted him by a grateful Parliament, Cromwell remarked sarcastically that he would give no votes to men 'that have no interest but the interest of breathing.'

A compromise was reached, the 'Agreement' finally proposing a vote for veteran soldiers, but not for wage-earners or beggars. Cromwell had seen the realities of English power politics with uncanny clarity. Democracy as the young men in his army dreamed of could be dangerous.

Puritanical strictness was beginning to irk ordinary people, and the long-drawn-out war had exasperated them. Had every Englishman in 1647 been given a free vote in a democratic election, there is little doubt whatever that King Charles, though a prisoner, would have won by an immense majority.

The Army Council's debates at Putney were followed by a lively Christmas. In London, soldiers had to be ordered out to stop apprentices from decorating a pump in Cornhill with holly and ivy, and at Canterbury, in Kent, there was a huge riot. A Puritan mayor tried to forbid a football match that by tradition took place every Christmas in the market place. Three thousand men of the trained bands had at last to be called in to restore order in the turbulent little town.

After Parliament's decree that London theatres should close their doors, plays had been given in secret, sometimes by puppet theatres. But in January 1648 the ordinance forbidding stage plays expired and, by an oversight in some government office, was not renewed. The London theatre sprang to life at once.

At the Bull they were playing Beaumont and Fletcher's *Wit without Words* to packed houses. A hundred and twenty coaches put down passengers at the Fortune Theatre on the night of 27 January. But on 11 February Parliament struck: stage plays were once more forbidden. Orders were given to destroy the seating in every London theatre. Spectators at plays were to be fined, and every actor publicly flogged.

On 9 April came the biggest riot of all.

Playing games on the Sabbath was forbidden. Some boys broke this rule in Moorfields one Sunday, and the Lord Mayor ordered soldiers to go and stop them. London's apprentice lads would not stand by and see this happen. They pelted the soldiers with stones, and set all London in an uproar.

The furious apprentices had long been deprived of their holiday fun by the puritanical Lord Mayor and Aldermen in whose cause they had often fought. They were angry too because these same rich men were using their new freedom of action to ride roughshod over medieval customs that promised them fair wages once they were journeymen and a chance at last to set up on their own.

A mob of five thousand, including many old soldiers, came surging along the Strand to cries of 'Now for King Charles!' They were going to drive the New Model soldiers out of Whitehall.

But this was easier said than done. Oliver Cromwell himself led a charge of Ironsides down the Strand against them and two civilians were killed.

The furious apprentices seized Ludgate and Newgate. The Lord Mayor, well knowing he was detested, took refuge in the Tower of London, and by eight next morning the apprentices controlled the City. But for all their bravery and war experience they were part-time soldiers, no match for the Ironsides.

A thousand New Model infantry and three hundred troopers marched around London and smashed their way in by the back door, through Moorgate. Cromwell put the leaders of the rebel apprentices in prison and garrisoned the Tower with his own men.

There was not much doubt by now who held the real power in England.

Royalists living in London and the counties nearby had been obliged all through the war so far to keep their heads down and walk discreetly. They felt particularly frustrated at not having done their share in the royal cause, and even after Naseby there were men among them keen to fight on.

New hope had been given these diehard Cavaliers earlier in the winter, when King Charles managed to escape from his captivity at Hampton Court, where he had been too closely watched to hatch any effective plots for a Royalist uprising. There were also rumours that the notorious Colonel Harrison, the butcher's son, was planning to assassinate the King. So one day Charles took his chance and rode off for the south coast.

On the road Charles debated in his mind whether to stay in England and plot an insurrection with his friends, or take a ship to France and join Henrietta Maria. But when the King got near Southampton an embargo on all shipping bound for France forced the decision on him. He then took the advice of John Ashburnham and went across to Carisbrooke Castle on the Isle of Wight, expecting that the Governor, Colonel Hammond, would treat him leniently.

Hammond was also, as it happened, a distant relative of Cromwell – who at once brought pressure to bear. The conscientious young soldier was torn between sympathy with the King and his duty to Parliament. In the end, Charles was once more locked up and closely watched. But for quite long enough, Carisbrooke Castle had been the centre of a great spider's web of Royalist conspiracy.

Some threads reached to France, where Henrietta Maria, ever undaunted, was pawning her personal jewels to buy yet more arms. Other threads linked up the many English counties where loyal Cavaliers awaited their second chance. Some threads reached to Scotland, to the Duke of Hamilton and others like him who detested the power and radical opinions of the New Model Army. The Scots, with the secret connivance of Presbyterians in the English Parliament, were getting an army ready to invade England once again and this time impose a Presbyterian system there by force.

But by provoking another civil war, Charles was destroying the real basis of his personal power. He was a force to be reckoned with, even when in prison, because of the sympathy he received from so many of his own people. But now, above all else, ordinary people craved peace in the land.

King Charles, as his plot thickened, still carried on make-believe peace negotiations with both Army and Parliament, often managing cleverly to play one off against the other. At last Oliver Cromwell felt obliged to warn King Charles bluntly that unless he came to terms with the Army pretty soon, there was nothing to stop them from crowning the young Duke of York as King James II.

James, by now a lad of sixteen, was living under careful guard with his younger brother and sister in St James's Palace. To Parliament the three royal youngsters were valuable pawns in the chess game of political power. The King sent a message to a cool-headed and faithful Royalist called Colonel John Bamfield, asking him to rescue young James, and saying 'I look upon James's escape as Charles's preservation, and nothing can content me more.'

Colonel Bamfield got word to the royal children, telling them exactly what to do. In St James's Palace, hide-and-seek became the craze, until everyone got so used to seeing James and the younger children running in and out of their apartments and hiding from sight that if one of them 'disappeared' for half an hour the guards took no particular notice.

Anne Murray, a lady-in-waiting, took young James's measurements and went to a tailor to order a woman's costume for him. (The tailor happened to remark that never in his working life had he encountered so tall a girl with so thick a waist!)

On the evening of 20 April 1648, Colonel Bamfield smuggled young James the key of a small door set in a wall of the palace gardens. The usual game of hide-and-seek began, and this time big brother hid in the garden. James was through the garden door, into a waiting coach, and muffled up in a woman's cloak and wig long before the waiting guards began to wonder when the game would end.

In a house nearby, Anne Murray dressed the young prince in a mohair gown with a scarlet underpetticoat, and assured him that he made a very pretty girl. On his way out to the ship in the river, James passed himself off as Colonel Bamfield's sister, and got away by sea to Holland only an hour or so before an emergency order arrived closing all the ports in the kingdom.

CHAPTER ELEVEN

The Power of the Sword

All you intended when you set us a-fighting was merely to unhorse and dismount our old riders and tyrants, that you might get up and ride us in their stead – JOHN LILBURNE

> I'll sing thine obsequies with trumpet sounds
> And write thine epitaph in blood and wounds.
> – JAMES GRAHAM, Marquess of Montrose,
> on hearing of the death of King Charles I

WILLIAM BATTEN, the senior naval officer who had bombarded Queen Henrietta Maria both coming and going, was a convinced Presbyterian, so he intensely disliked the way the Army was gaining the upper hand in the kingdom. In October 1647, Batten was detected in a plot to sail to Scotland with twenty-two warships to join the Covenanters. The royal conspiracy had reached out a long way and involved the fleet.

Seamen of the navy had all been enthusiastic for Parliament when the Civil War began. They had marched through London, cheering the Five Members. But their pay too was now badly in arrears, and since they were nearly always at sea, the Army's democratic ideas had scarcely touched them.

Earlier in his life Colonel Rainsborough had been a sea-captain. When Batten was dismissed, the chance was seized to get a notorious Leveller out of the Army by sending Rainsborough to command the fleet. This was not a good idea. Soldiers and sailors at the best of times have no great love for one another, and many naval officers detested Rainsborough's radical opinions.

William Batten made his headquarters in Hoop Tavern,

Leadenhall Street, and cunningly masterminded a mutiny against Thomas Rainsborough. Seamen from the fleet were won over with generous treats of free beer, and their officers whispered solemn warnings that Colonel. Rainsborough's arrival was only a start. Hundreds of soldiers would soon be sent aboard, to take over all the best jobs in the ships-of-war.

The sailors were then brought ashore to hear a clever young imposter called Cornelius Evans, who had landed in Sandwich from the Low Countries and managed to pass himself off as the Prince of Wales. On the Kentish coast six warships declared for King Charles. Their ship's companies took possession of the castles at Deal, Sandown, and Walmer, and blockaded Dover.

The mutiny in the fleet was the signal awaited by the King's friends all over England. Nearby in Kent there was a popular uprising against Puritan rule, in which Cavaliers who had been biding their time took the lead. In places all over England where the King had friends similar outbreaks followed.

In Kent the insurrection at first swept all before it. A crowd of 'Cavaliers, seamen, citizens and watermen' came out from London to join the Kentish rebels; many were ordinary Londoners who had turned against the Puritans at last and were siding now with King Charles. By 26 May 1648, the King's men had a battery of guns mounted at Deptford to command ships sailing up the Thames. Seven thousand Kentish insurrectionaries, mostly poor countrymen but all heart and soul for King Charles, met on Penenden Heath to choose a general.

Lord Fairfax – Black Tom had recently inherited his father's title – was by this time a sick man, racked by gout and kidney stones. But Kent was dangerously close to London, and he met the Cavalier threat to the capital with a typical burst of feverish and brilliantly directed energy.

Soldiers from the New Model Army had been sent quickly all over England, to patrol danger spots or put down local risings, so Fairfax was left at that critical moment with only 8,000 men. He soon had them on the march, nudging the Cavaliers and their guns out of Deptford, and moving skilfully across country to bottle up most of the rebel army at Maidstone.

Command of the Kent rising had been given to Lord Norwich, the old courtier who before the war had drawn his income from the scandalous sugar-and-butter monopoly. In an armed encounter against the best fighting men in Europe, led by Black Tom Fairfax, and a courageous armed mob led by an ageing court favourite, the Kentish men would hardly stand a chance, yet they fought marvellously, and in Maidstone 'every street was got by inches'.

Driven by Fairfax out of Maidstone, Lord Norwich rode his 500 cavalry towards the eastern suburbs of London. They swam their horses across the Thames at Stratford-at-Bow and waited there three days, in the hope that friends inside London might open the City gates for them. But old Philip Skippon had already manned the gates with volunteers loyal to Parliament, and since the apprentices' riot in April, the streets of London were policed by Ironsides.

Many Londoners had turned their sympathies towards King Charles, but few were willing to risk their lives hopelessly in his cause. The Royalist rising had most success in those counties that so far had had little direct experience of war. Only a handful of King's men – apprentices, men from the waterfront, royal veterans – came out of London to join Lord Norwich and his Cavaliers at Stratford.

Norwich moved towards unplundered East Anglia, so as to strike a blow at the Puritan heartland, but near Chelmsford he met with Sir Charles Lucas riding at the head of the Essex Cavaliers. Lucas, a cool-headed soldier of great ex-

perience, warned Lord Norwich that Fairfax was close on
their tail. In a forced march of fifty hours, Black Tom had
moved 5,000 of his men fifty miles.

The Cavaliers wheeled their chargers and made for the
small walled city of Colchester. If they could only compel
Fairfax and his 5,000 to besiege them in Colchester, the
Royalist insurrection elsewhere in England would stand a
chance – and besides, the Scots were coming.

Sir Charles Lucas took command. Outside the city walls
he drew up his 4,000 men in battle array. The foot, in the
centre, barred the Ironsides' way down the London road,
and the Cavaliers guarded the flanks. Some of his volunteers,
enthusiastic youngsters from London, had never handled
weapons before. Yet with Sir Charles to lead them they re-
pelled three successive charges by the Ironside brigade under
Colonel Barkstead, the New Model force that until recently
had been employed to police London.

Sir Charles then quietly ordered his men to feign defeat.
His little army, as if three Ironside charges had been enough,
withdrew through Head Gate into Colchester. Barkstead
could see that the Cavaliers as they backed away from him
had left the city gate undone. He ordered his Ironsides to
rush Head Gate and they galloped headlong into a trap.

Sir Charles Lucas, who had gone into action that day
carrying only a walking cane, had his Cavaliers waiting at the
top of the sloping street. At a signal from Sir Charles they
charged towards the gate, taking the Ironsides head on, while
files of musketeers, posted up a side street, fired with murderous effect into their flank. This was not quite such easy
work for Barkstead's men as riding down and sabreing unarmed Londoners. The Ironsides turned and fled.

Head Gate was locked by means of a peg, and the peg
was missing. With a typically Cavalier gesture, Sir Charles
Lucas fastened the gate with the walking cane he had car-

ried into battle. Although Colchester was Sir Charles's hometown, most of the citizens there were Puritan. Quickly the Cavaliers organized Colchester to stand a siege. As Fairfax tried in vain to storm the city's ancient walls, word came to him that a large Scottish army was poised to invade England's northern border. This army had been raised by a group of Scots noblemen under the influence of the Duke of Hamilton. The Kirk had misgivings about this invasion and had done little to help recruitment, so that this time the Scottish soldiers who entered England were not high-minded psalm-singers, but rogues.

At this desperate moment, Oliver Cromwell and his men were besieging Pembroke Castle on the far side of Wales. The Welsh countryside was so hostile to Roundheads that Cromwell could hardly find a blacksmith to shoe his cavalry chargers. Nor could he make a breach in the wall of Pembroke Castle, because the boat carrying all his siege artillery had sunk when it crossed the River Severn.

But Hugh Peter, the ex-minister from Salem, Massachusetts, rode off full tilt to Milford Haven and borrowed four guns from the armament of the warship *Lion*. Pembroke Castle fell to the Ironsides, and the insurgent Welsh were soon battered into submission. Fairfax and his men were pinned down at Colchester, but Oliver Cromwell was free to march against the Scots.

Cromwell described his men in a letter as 'so harassed by long marches they seemed rather fit for a hospital than a battle.' Many were marching barefoot, but though none had been paid lately, they never once plundered the poor countryman. On this way northward through Nottingham, Cromwell picked up 2,500 pairs of shoes, which eased their plight somewhat.

John Lilburne, spokesman for the Levellers, was held in a London prison. In Parliament and the City the Presbyterians well knew that Lilburne's followers had been at odds with Ireton and Cromwell over 'The Agreement of the People'. If Lilburne and his Levellers would only go on attacking Cromwell, that would weaken the New Model Army's morale. So at this crisis they set John Lilburne free, and even paid him money. The Presbyterians would not have been sorry to see the Scots army reach London.

Lilburne decided instead to put all his great influence behind Cromwell until the Scots were defeated, and he wrote to tell Cromwell so. Political discussion among the soldiers was over, and differences were temporarily forgotten. Only the marching feet of the Army could stamp out the spreading flames of this war.

The Scots and their English Cavalier allies were moving down through the northern counties in a leisurely and disordered fashion, plundering as they came. By the time Cromwell reached Otley in Yorkshire and joined forces with the local Roundheads, he had 8,000 men. The Scots, once their sprawling army was concentrated, would have nearly 30,000.

On crossing the Border, the Duke of Hamilton had announced that the Scots were entering England for 'settling Presbyterian government according to the Covenant.' Wasn't this what those English Roundheads had all sworn? According to the Scots, the Roundheads had failed to keep their oath.

Once the repressive control of the Kirk ministers was lifted from their army, the Scots acted like bandits. The Duke's scallywag followers ran the sheep and cattle off the northern moors, robbed poor cottagers of everything they possessed, and held children for ransom. If the terrified parents did not at once pay a cash ransom, the child was struck dead.

Their sprawling line of march extended for fifty miles,

and this gave Cromwell his chance. To enter Lancashire, where King Charles still had many friends, Hamilton's army would have to cross the bridge over the Ribble at Preston. Cromwell decided to march his men along the north bank of the Ribble and, by taking that bridge, cut the Scots army in two.

Gaunt and grim Sir Marmaduke Langdale, who had fought Cromwell at Naseby, was commanding the 3,000 English Cavaliers and 600 royal foot who had joined forces with Hamilton. On 16 August, these North Country Royalists fought an obstinate delaying action along the sunken lane leading into Preston. The year 1648 had been the wettest summer in memory, and the mud was deep. At first Hamilton could hardly believe that Oliver Cromwell's army was so close, and when the news was confirmed that Langdale and Cromwell were fighting in the mud and rain outside Preston, he exclaimed 'Let them alone. The English dogs are but killing one another.'

Sir Marmaduke Langdale's dour infantry had to be pushed back step by step in bloody frontal charges before Cromwell's men could break through to Preston. To seize the bridge there cost them another two hours of repeated pike attacks. But the Scots army was cut in half and the odds reduced. And hundreds of Lancashire men who years before had fought with Colonel Rigby and had been shocked by the conduct of the Scots soldiers were coming in to join Cromwell as volunteers.

Cromwell left them to garrison Preston and guard his rear. His enemy was spread out and off guard. The Scots cavalry vanguard was busy plundering Wigan fifteen miles to the south, even though Wigan was a Royalist town.

Cromwell rode his men hard through darkness and drenching rain to destroy the half of the Scots army that was now in his power. All that night and the next day his cavalry killed fugitives with the sword until they were sick of killing. Here and there a group of Scots soldiers under a good officer would make a stand against the terrible Ironsides, but half of Hamilton's men had already thrown away their weapons. They had not eaten for two days and, when made prisoner, were so demoralized that ten Roundheads were enough to keep a thousand of them from running away. Three thousand of the invading Scots army were killed in that merciless pursuit and ten thousand taken prisoner. Hamilton and his cavalry surrendered on 24 August, five days after the infantry had given up.

In that wet October of 1648 the Ironside officers, led by Cromwell again found a way of making a cash profit from their victory. Pressed men taken captive were sent back home to Scotland, on their promise never again to join an army invading England. But both Scots and English volunteers, those heartwhole Royalists who had followed the Duke of Hamilton from conviction, were sold off as slaves. Some were sent out to plantations in Virginia or Barbados, others shipped as galley slaves to Venice. And officers who had fought well were rewarded with the purchase price.

In his message to Parliament giving the good news of victory at Preston, Oliver Cromwell bluntly demanded that 'they that are implacable and will not leave troubling the land may be speedily destroyed.' His message was a threat aimed directly at King Charles.

By this time in Colchester, the inhabitants were eating the rotten carcasses of cavalry chargers, and a dead lapdog sold for six shillings. The mayor of Colchester pleaded with Lord Fairfax to let the starving women and children leave the town, but Fairfax refused. The war, by dragging on so long, had warped his chivalrous nature; even Fairfax had turned ruthless.

Sir Charles Lucas, glad to have fewer mouths to feed, opened the city gate for the hungry women and children and gave them a chance to run towards the Parliamentary lines. Most were from families that had sympathized with Parliament. But Fairfax told his troops to halt them by firing over their heads.

The women of Colchester were told that if they came closer they would be stripped of all their clothes by the soldiers, to shame them, and sent back into the city naked. The women and their children spent a hungry and frightened night between the dread Ironside enemy and the high town walls, until at daybreak Sir Charles, taking pity, opened the town gate for them again.

When word came of Oliver Cromwell's victory at Preston, Sir Charles Lucas and Lord Norwich yielded up Colchester. For the Royalists, everything had hinged on the Scots invasion, and it had failed. This time, even though his enemy had yielded, Lord Fairfax, 'his mouth drawn all awry with pain', displayed no mercy.

Sir Charles Lucas and Sir George Lisle were picked from among the Cavalier leaders to be shot out of hand as an example. They were led before a firing squad of six dragoons in the castle keep. Sir George jestingly told the dragoons to come closer, saying 'I have been nearer to you when you missed me.' As the squad turned their carbines to aim at Sir Charles, he exclaimed boldly 'Remember me to all my friends – and tell them I have died in a good cause!'

A cash profit was made, too, from the surrender at Colchester. Gentlemen volunteers were shared as plunder among the Roundhead officers, either to be ransomed by their families or sold off as galley slaves. Junior officers and private soldiers were crowded into Colchester church, stripped down to their shirts, and then marched barefoot to ports in the West Country. Those who fainted on the road were instantly shot dead. The survivors were then sold off, most of them as slaves to the American plantations, some to the galleys in Venice.

The Civil War had begun for freedom, but by an ugly paradox it was culminating in slavery.

Late in November 1648, General Ireton and John Lilburne had a frank discussion. Ireton was speaking for his father-in-law, Oliver Cromwell, who for the time being would have been glad to go on getting political support from Lilburne and his Levellers. Cromwell was seeking temporary allies because he intended to attack first the Presbyterians in Parliament, and then King Charles. But Freeborn John saw through this scheme and reached the shrewd conclusion that the grandees of the army were planning to set up a military dictatorship.

The grandees had prospered from the war, and their principles had triumphed, but they knew they would always be a small and unpopular minority. Even the most tolerant and intelligent among the Independents were never likely to win the hearts of ordinary people. King Charles was more popular, but in a military sense he now had no chance of winning, either. The Cromwellians on the Army Council had already rejected their men's demand for a Leveller democracy, so their one remaining option was to govern England by force of arms. Government by brute force is the only real alternative to government by consent.

Not long after, Colonel Harrison told Lilburne frankly that the Army's leaders had decided amongst themselves to put the King to death, by court-martial, if necessary.

John Lilburne himself valued personal freedom above all else. He had wanted to see the Civil War lead to a society where no man would 'be questioned or molested or put to answer for anything but wherein he materially violates the person, goods or good name of another.' The Levellers, said Lilburne, rather than sacrifice the King, would 'keep up one tyrant to balance another' – that is, keep King Charles alive and influential, as a countervailing power, if the alternative should be to 'devolve all the government of the Kingdom into the wills and swords of the army.'

Cromwell had, step by step, been coming closer to an inner conviction that there was no other way to govern England according to the principles he thought good – indeed, divinely inspired – but by an autocratic power, based on the sword, and exercised according to his personal will.

Cromwell was a profoundly religious man, and decisions that his political enemies have, at times, been tempted to interpret as self-interested or even hypocritical were usually reached after fervent prayers for divine guidance.

Some may consider a tyrant who announces that he is doing the will of God as an unconscious blasphemer. Others may find in him a splendid embodiment of historical destiny. Intelligent and honest men have seen Oliver Cromwell in both these guises, and it must be frankly admitted that Cromwell was far from being history's worst or most outrageous dictator.

He sincerely intended to do good. He was a great soldier, and a man of outstanding practical ability. He was uncommonly tolerant of those who opposed his will on inessential matters. When he was cruel, as in Ireland, he appears to have acted from cold policy rather than from a hardened habit of wickedness.

But John Lilburne did not wish to see even the best of dictators rule England by the sword. When Cromwell succeeded in gaining the supreme power for which he was now clearly striving, what would happen to the human liberty for which Lilburne and brave young men like him had so generously shed their blood?

To rule by the sword, the army grandees must begin by getting rid of their Presbyterian enemies in Parliament. Seven years before, when the war began, those godly, prosperous, drably dressed middle-aged men who sat with Pym and Hampden on the firelit benches in St Stephen's had been able to call upon thousands of eager volunteers to take their part against the King.

This enthusiastic support for Parliament in the streets of London had now been lost – to the King, or else to Lilburne's radical democracy. The power of the men in Parliament was a fiction.

On 6 December 1648, at seven in the morning, Colonel Pride of the New Model Army, who had begun his life driving a horse and wagon, filled the approaches to Parliament with soldiers. He stood there in the lobby with a list in his hand. The Reverend Hugh Peter from Massachusetts stood at his side. Chaplains never go armed, but that day Hugh Peter wore a sword. On Colonel Pride's list were 143 names of members considered hostile to the Army.

Ninety-six Members of Parliament let themselves be turned away at the door without a protest. Forty-five who made a fuss were locked up, the soldiers as they manhandled them saying disrespectfully 'These are the men who have cozened the State of our money, and kept back our pay.' When one member demanded to know by what authority he was made prisoner, Hugh Peter slapped the weapon at his side and answered stridently 'By the power of the sword.'

On the night of 17 December, the drawbridge of gloomy Hurst Castle, where the King had been kept a close prisoner, was lowered to let in a party of troopers and dragoons. King Charles at first thought they had been sent to murder him, but they were his escort to London.

A New Model colonel arrived to take charge, 'gallantly mounted and armed, a velvet montero was on his head, a new buffcoat upon his back, and a crimson silk scarf round his waist, richly fringed.' This was Colonel Harrison, the notorious extremist. Harrison laughingly denied the long-standing rumours that he had come to assassinate King Charles. Indeed, the King rather liked him.

On 21 December, a Royalist secret agent called John Law-rans reported that Cromwell had begun to fall out with the Levellers, 'his designs and theirs being as incompatible as fire and water, they driving at a pure democracy and himself at an oligarchy.' Oliver Cromwell, confided the report, was now sleeping 'in one of the King's rich beds at Whitehall.'

The power of the sword was astonishing. Parliament had been dispersed. The Levellers, simple men fond of argu-ment, would not be difficult to crush. And once King Charles was safely dead, Oliver Cromwell was well aware that no-thing else would stand between himself and absolute power. He would claim to exercise that power in accordance with God's will. But it would be power, none the less.

A hundred and thirty-five commissioners were handpicked to act as both judge and jury in the trial of King Charles. Even Puritan lawyers had opposed the proceedings as illegal. Harry Vane, Cromwell's closest political ally during the difficult years, refused in silent protest to take his seat in the House of Commons between 6 December 1648, the day of Pride's Purge, and 7 February 1649. But an ambitious lawyer of no great distinction called John Bradshaw was found willing to serve as president of the court.

When the commissioners first met at the Painted Chamber in Whitehall, Cromwell, Fairfax, and Ireton were among them, with seven New Model colonels, and the republicans

Ludlow and Marten. But only forty others of the 135 turned up, and after the first time, Lord Fairfax never put in another appearance.

Black Tom Fairfax had parted company with his own soldiers at last. This threat to Charles disturbed him deeply, as it did John Lilburne, but the army's rank and file were happy to be offered a scapegoat. After the bloodshed at Colchester, and Preston, the soldiers of the New Model Army were very willing to believe Oliver Cromwell when he told them there could be no peace in the land while 'Charles Stuart, that man of blood' still drew breath. The soldiers wanted peace; they wanted to go home. Over tankards of ale in London taverns, Ironsides were loudly telling each other 'Stone dead hath no fellow!'

On 20 January 1649, Charles was brought from St James's Palace to Westminster. Lest people might cheer him as he passed in the street, he was transported to his trial in a curtained sedan-chair, and then by boat. The commissioners who were to judge him sat on a raised dais at one end of Westminster Hall, their seats and benches hung with scarlet. Only sixty-eight of them had taken their places.

Armed soldiers kept the crowd of onlookers well away from the judges. Distinguished visitors took their seats in the two corner galleries. This was the direction from which trouble might come. The judges kept their hats on throughout the trial, and for fear of assassination John Bradshaw wore a hat with a bulletproof lining.

Proceedings began with commissioners answering to their names. When the name 'Lord Fairfax!' was called, a masked woman in the gallery cried out 'He has more wit than to be here!'

King Charles was brought in through a side door to face his accusers. He wore a dark suit and over it a cloak that partly hid the great star of the Garter glittering on his breast.

He carried a white cane with a silver head. Observing that the judges had no intention of taking their hats off to him, he kept his own hat on, and from then on showed no deference to the court.

A red-upholstered chair had been set out for the King. As he went across to take his seat, the silver head fell off his cane and rolled across the polished floor. All through Charles's life there had been royal servants only too eager to wait on him. Now nobody stooped to oblige him. After a brief, ironic pause, the King reached down and picked up the silver knob for himself.

The indictment was read. On hearing himself described as a 'traitor', King Charles burst out laughing. The formal accusation against the King was in the name of 'the people of England'. At these words the masked woman in the gallery spoke out once more in her loud, clear voice.

'It is a lie! Not a half or a quarter of the people of England! Oliver Cromwell is a traitor!'

Colonel Daniel Axtell, commanding the guard, ordered his men to fire their carbines into the gallery. The soldiers were slow to obey, and before the threat was carried out the intrepid Lady Fairfax had made her escape.

Charles was usually a shy and reserved man, with a slight speech impediment, but this time, as he began to speak in his own defence, his stutter miraculously left him.

'It is not my case alone,' the King told the court, in answer to their indictment, 'it is the freedom and liberty of the people of England, and do you pretend what you will, I stand more for their liberties; for if power without law may make laws, may alter the fundamental laws of the kingdom, I do not know what subject he is in England may be sure of his life, or of anything that he calls his own.'

Charles was doomed to die. His trial was being held in public only in the hope of somehow making English people believe that the death of their King was justified. But from the very first moment, Charles's simple courage turned opinion in his favour. Never again in the trial, after that first speech, was he given a chance to answer his accusers at length.

By the night of 26 January only twenty-eight of the judges had signed the death warrant, Cromwell's name being third and John Okey's sixth. Henry Marten, the republican, and Oliver Cromwell signed the warrant and then, in nervous high spirits, went on to splash each other's faces with ink, like naughty schoolboys. Less than half of the handpicked judges had turned up at the trial, and less than a fifth were prepared of their own free will to put their names to a sentence of death.

The commissioners attending court on the last day were tricked into standing up as a public sign that they agreed to the sentence, whether as individuals they had yet put their signatures to the death warrant or not. Bradshaw refused to give King Charles a chance to answer his judges. As the crowd in the court began spontaneously to shout 'God save the King!' Colonel Axtell ordered his soldiers to drown their voices by roaring out 'Justice!' The King was dragged away by force, protesting aloud 'If I am not suffered to speak, expect what justice other people will have!'

Cromwell finally managed to bully fifty-nine judges out of the original 135 into signing the death warrant. Nine of those attending the trial refused to submit to him, and never did sign. An armed watch was put on Black Tom Fairfax, in case he might be tempted to rescue the King. To save his father's life, the young Prince of Wales sent Parliament, or what was left of it, a blank piece of paper bearing his signature. On it Charles's opponents could write their own terms. The gesture was rejected. Cromwell was out for blood.

On the morning of 29 January 1649, Charles was allowed

for the last time to see his two captive children, the thirteen-year-old Elizabeth and nine-year-old Henry. The King, in tears, took them on his knee and told them he was about to die a glorious death 'for the laws and liberties of this land, and for the true Protestant religion.' He had forgiven, he said, all his enemies, and hoped that God, too, would forgive them.

Charles warned little Henry solemnly not to let himself be placed on the vacant throne as a puppet king. Elizabeth was to tell her mother 'that his thoughts had never strayed from her, and that his love should be the same to the last.' Then the King divided his personal jewellery between the two children as keepsakes.

The morning of 30 January, the day of execution, was frosty. King Charles put on two shirts, explaining to his chaplain 'The season is so sharp as probably may make me shake, which some observers may imagine proceeds from fear. Death is not terrible to me. I bless my God I am prepared.'

Charles walked through the Banqueting Hall of Whitehall, under the painted ceiling he had commissioned from Rubens, and out to the scaffold in the open air accompanied by William Juxon, the Anglican bishop of London.

Around the timber scaffold, Ironsides had been drawn up on horseback in ranks so deep that the vast crowd of patiently waiting Londoners would be unable to hear the King's voice. Charles therefore repeated to the bishop what he had intended to say to the crowd. These last words, as reported by Bishop Juxon, give the clearest expression to the real difference between King and Parliament, the fundamental disagreement about the way to govern England, which at last had sent King Charles to the scaffold.

'For the people, truly I desire their liberty and freedom,' Charles told the bishop, 'as much as anybody whatsoever, but I must tell you that their liberty and freedom consists in having government, those laws by which their lives and their goods may be most their own. It is not their having a share in the government; that is nothing appertaining unto them. A subject and a sovereign are clean different things.'

The King's human sympathy had been broadened by his war experiences, but from first to last, his principles had never changed. As Charles saw it, even at that last moment of his life, the responsibility of governing the realm of England had been placed on his shoulders by God, and this Divine Right he would neither yield nor share.

The King knelt at the block in prayer. He then stretched out his hands as a signal to the masked executioner. The glittering axe fell. The masked man stooped to lift up the King's severed head for the entire waiting crowd to see. At the executioner's traditional cry, 'Behold the head of a traitor!', a huge groan of horror and anger broke from the watching Londoners. Two troops of cavalry promptly turned their horses' heads outwards and patrolled threateningly up and down Whitehall hand on sword hilt, to disperse the crowd to their homes.

Later that year, Oliver Cromwell succeeded with great political astuteness in crushing by armed force the last of his rivals for power, the Levellers. Their dream of a democratic England, where every man would vote into power a truly representative Parliament, and where the land would no longer be the hereditary property of a rich and often aristocratic few, was not yet practical politics. But in the English-speaking world on both sides of the Atlantic it remained a cherished dream.

The material temptations inducing the Army's grandees to accept a dictatorship after a war that had been fought to extend freedom can be illustrated from the case of John

Okey, the Baptist colonel of dragoons, though in the end Okey too came to mistrust and oppose Cromwell. In 1649, the stocky London drayman, who had fought all the way from Edgehill to Naseby, helped Cromwell to crush by force the Army's Levellers when they made their last stand at Burford. He was given in gratitude a degree by Oxford University, from which all but Puritans had lately been expelled. Cromwell saw to it not long after that Okey got £300 a year from the forfeited estates of Scots Royalists.

As a colonel, Okey had been receiving £63 a month, or over sixty times the pay of an infantryman. His dragoons were paid their arrears in debentures, issued against the security of Church or Crown lands. Senior officers would often cash these valuable documents for their men at about a quarter of their face value. By some such means, John Okey, now a Justice of the Peace as well as a Master of Arts, acquired three manors, a country mansion in Bedfordshire, and a handsome town house in London, a long way from his little shop on Tower Hill.

Black Tom Fairfax retired to his Yorkshire estates, a sick man, to write poetry – bad, but his own – and enjoy the sight of flowers and children and animals. Fairfax had always been an honest fighting soldier, out of his depth in politics, but once Cromwell had made himself supremely powerful as Lord Protector in 1653, Fairfax gave his support to those intriguing to bring back the Prince of Wales as King Charles II.

The young prince had already begun to show that, unlike his father, he would probably assent to the vast changes the Civil War had made in property, laws, and religion. But so long as Oliver Cromwell lived and his Puritan dictatorship lasted, the prospect that England one day might have a constitutional King remained a dream.

The soldiers' hopes of going home in peace once the King

was dead were not realized either. The New Model Army was shipped overseas, to crush the independent national government set up by the Catholic Irish – a military task the Ironsides accomplished with such gruesome efficiency that 'the Curse of Cromwell on you' is still an Irish oath.

The speculators in London and Edinburgh got their grip on vast Irish estates, and some land-hungry New Model soldiers procured farms there. Cromwell's policy of 'Hell or Connaught!' originated a method for dealing with the native Irish not unlike that later applied to the American Indians. Either they made the extreme far west of Ireland their reservation, or they faced extinction. From first to last, the war cost Ireland two-fifths of her people.

A hundred thousand Englishmen were killed in action in the Civil War out of a population of five million. Proportionately this loss was even greater than England endured in the bloodletting of the First World War. Many more died of wounds, sickness, and hunger; it was a long, hard war.

In the year that King Charles – known to his admirers ever since as King Charles the Martyr – died with such dignity on the scaffold, a man called George Fox began preaching. What he had to say went home to thousands who had fought and suffered on the Puritan side in the war. By 1665 Fox had 80,000 followers. They were nicknamed Quakers, and many of them were former soldier radicals, including Freeborn John Lilburne, in the distant island prison to which Cromwell had sent him.

The thousands of Roundhead veterans who joined George Fox's Society of Friends renounced the sword. Having failed to achieve brotherhood on earth by armed force or democratic process, they looked for a mystical fraternity in religion. They rejected the official church, the authority of the state, war taxation, and all vestiges of social inequality. Of course they were persecuted, and many English Quakers had to cross the Atlantic, where they colonized Pennsylvania.

A good many Cavaliers also fled from Cromwell's dictatorship to America, usually to Virginia. The forebears of Washington, Madison and Lee all arrived in Virginia as Royalist refugees.

When Cromwell died in 1658 and a chance came to restore King Charles II to his father's throne, the new King pardoned all those who had fought against the royal cause, except the men who had actually condemned his father to death. Sir Harry Vane and thirteen regicides were executed.

Twenty-four of Charles's judges had already died. Even the dead did not wholly escape. The bones of Cromwell, Ireton, Pride, and Bradshaw were dug up and reburied at the foot of the gallows at Tyburn.

In 1660 Edward Whalley, who had commanded the second line of Ironsides at Naseby and later signed the King's death warrant, fled with another Cromwellian general, William Goffe, three thousand miles across the sea to Boston.

When two royal officers arrived the following year to arrest them, they moved to Connecticut and found refuge in New Haven in the house of the Reverend John Davenport. That Sunday the minister preached a sermon to the good people of New Haven from Isaiah 16.3–4: 'Hide the outcasts, bewray not him that wandereth. Let mine outcasts dwell with thee.' His congregation, who had seen the two strangers arrive in town, took the hint.

For a month they hid the regicides in a nearby cave, sending a small boy to them by night with food. When the hue and cry died down, Whalley and Goffe moved to Milford, Massachusetts, where for two years they stayed indoors, never showing their faces. At last they sought safety for the rest of their lives a hundred miles nearer the wilderness, at

Hadley, then a frontier settlement. And there, when a very old man, Major-General William Goffe of the New Model Army came out of hiding when an Indian uprising began, to show the settlers from his old experience how a war should be fought.

Democrats and Cavaliers alike took their beliefs with them to America. The long civil struggle in England then and later was the seedbed from which in time the American Constitution and the Bill of Rights were to grow to full bloom.

When King Charles II came to the throne in 1660, John Okey, like others who had signed the death warrant, was sent to the block. But old Roundheads were usually more fortunate, and most managed to keep the estates they had amassed in the war. With Charles I dead, many medieval legal obstacles to buying land, engaging in trade, or under-paying wage-earners became obsolete. Buying and selling were unfettered, and this, in the eyes of an acquisitive few, was precisely the freedom for which the war had been fought.

Others both in England and America had caught glimpses during the long war of a less self-centred view of human freedom, and a worthier democratic ideal. These sentiments they passed on to their children's children. When a new act of the historic drama opened in Boston in 1775, there were lovers of liberty on both sides of the Atlantic to applaud.

Bibliography

General reference

CLARENDON, EDWARD H., *Selections from the History of the Rebellion and Civil Wars and the Life by Himself.* London and New York, Oxford University Press, 1955. The complete history, by a statesman closely involved as the King's adviser, is a masterpiece – from the Cavalier point of view.

GARDINER, SAMUEL R., *History of the Great Civil War 1642–1649.* London, Longmans, 1893. A long and detailed history by a great authority; he has been slightly criticized lately for siding too much with Cromwell and not understanding the Levellers.

WEDGWOOD, CICELY V., *The King's War 1641–1647.* London, Collins, 1958. Rich in fascinating detail, the most interesting modern history for the ordinary reader.

WOOLRYCH, A. H., *Battles of the English Civil War.* London, Batsford, 1961. Gives a simplified and racy account of the political situation as interpreted by modern scholars.

Books about people

ASHLEY, MAURICE, *Cromwell's Generals.* London, Jonathan Cape, 1954.

BRETT, S. REED, *John Pym 1583–1643. The Statesman of the Puritan Revolution.* London, John Murray, 1940.

BUCHAN, JOHN, *Oliver Cromwell.* London, Hodder & Stoughton, 1934, and Westport, Connecticut, Greenwood Press, 1975.
Montrose. London, Thomas Nelson, 1928, and Mystic, Connecticut, Lawrence Verry, 1957. Both lively biographies by a great storyteller.

FERGUSSON, B., *Rupert of the Rhine*. London, Collins, 1952. Rupert as seen by a modern soldier who admires him.

FIRTH, SIR CHARLES, *Oliver Cromwell and the Rule of Puritans in England*. London and New York, Oxford University Press, 1953. Once authoritative but now a little out of date.

HILL, CHRISTOPHER, *God's Englishman: Oliver Cromwell and the English Revolution*. London and New York, Penguin Books, 1972. By the most eminent but most controversial living scholar of the period.

MILLER, PERRY, *Roger Williams: His Contribution to the American Tradition*. New York, Atheneum, 1962.

NEWCASTLE, DUCHESS OF, *Life of the First Duke of Newcastle*. London, Dent, 1915. A fascinating picture of the eccentric royalist leader by his wife.

WEDGWOOD, CICELY V., *The Trial of Charles I*. London, Collins, 1964.

Books about places

BROXAP, E., *The Great Civil War in Lancashire 1642–1651*. Manchester University Press, and Clifton, New Jersey, Kelley Publications, 1974.

COATES, ANN, *Cornwall in the Great Civil War and Interregnum 1642–1660*. Truro, D. B. Barton, 1963. The best and most interesting of the local histories.

PEARL, VALERIE, *London and the Outbreak of the Puritan Revolution*. London and New York, Oxford University Press, 1961. A detailed study that has changed our picture of what happened in London before war broke out.

Specialist studies

BRAILSFORD, H. N., *The Levellers and the English Revolution*. London, Cresset Press, 1961, and California, Stanford University Press, 1961.

BURNE, A. H., and YOUNG, P., *The Great Civil War 1642–1646*.

London, Eyre & Spottiswoode, 1959. A military history by two professional soldiers.

FIRTH, SIR CHARLES, *Cromwell's Army*. London, Methuen, 1962. How the New Model Army actually worked, in tactics, administration, etc.

ROGERS, H. C. B., *Battles and Generals of the Civil War*. London, Seeley Service, 1968. Another book by a professional soldier.

STONE, LAWRENCE, *The Causes of the English Revolution 1600–1660*. London, Routledge, Kegan Paul, and New York, Harper & Row, 1972. An excellent historian uses sociological techniques to upset ideas previously taken for granted.
The Crisis of Aristocracy 1558–1641. London, Oxford University Press, 1965, and New York, Oxford University Press, 1967. An important study that has changed our mental picture of the aristocracy.

YOUNG, P. and HOLMES, R., *The English Civil Wars 1642–1651: a Military History of Three Civil Wars*. London, Methuen, 1974.

Index

Also by James Barbary

THE BOER WAR

The Boers were amateur soldiers, and developed many ways of fighting that were then unusual in war. They became experts at guerrilla warfare – their small mobile forces attacked swiftly and then disappeared into a countryside they knew better than the enemy. The British fought back with a 'scorched earth' policy, and held many thousands of prisoners in their concentration camps – the 'invention' of Lord Kitchener. *The Boer War* tells of a conflict where more people were killed by sickness than by bullets, and women and children suffered as much as the soldiers; it goes on to show how the compromises of the peace treaty helped to bring about the problems South Africa faces to this day.

THE CRIMEAN WAR

Though British troops were probably the best-drilled and smartest in the world, the men at the top were not used to command. Administration broke down, the army was badly supplied with food and munitions, and the sick and wounded were neglected. For blunders, tactical errors and misunderstanding, the Crimean War has no equal in modern times. Of the 60,000 crack troops who left Britain in 1854, 43,000 were dead or disabled by January 1855. Only 7,000 had fallen in battle; cholera, exposure and starvation took care of the rest.

But the war did bring about enormous changes. It loosened the grip on the British Army of rich aristocrats who were soldiers because soldiering was fashionable. And the inspired sacrifice and hard work of Florençe Nightingale ensured that military hospitals at last became organized to *save* lives. The war also helped along the awakening of the Russian peasant from his long centuries of serfdom.

More Non-fiction in Puffins

QUIZZES AND PUZZLES

Alan Cash – The Puffin Crossword Puzzle Book
Norman and Margaret Dixon – The Puffin Quiz Book
Norman and Margaret Dixon – The Junior Puffin Quiz Book
Eric Emmet – The Puffin Book of Brainteasers
Michael Holt and Ronald Ridout – The Big Book of Puzzles
The Second Big Book of Puzzles
The Third Big Book of Puzzles
David Prole – The Puffin Soccer Quiz Book